This book is dedicated to all those who knew it made sense.

CONTENTS

★★★★★★★★★★★★★★★★★★★

PART ONE: WELCOME TO THE JUNGLE

PART TWO: BEING THE BOSS

Acknowledgements

I would like to thank all those that have inspired me at some time or another to be the best businessman that I can be; those without whom I could not have scaled the corporate peaks and firmly planted my flag.

Family and friends (you know who you are), Gordon Gekko, Ancient China, Theo Paphitis and God.

'If'

by Derek Trotter

If you can play it nice and cool while others
are sucking their thumbs and throwing a paddy,

If you can stand your ground, even when face to face with
a man-eating lion who's sizing you up for elevenses,

If you can put up with people when they're giving you the right
hump, and still be able to smile and bid them a fair *au revois*,

If you can feel equally at ease spending the weekend in the Duke
of Maylebury's west wing as you can kipping on Trigger's sofa,

If you can be the one who dared and thought of
this time next year when it all went belly up,

If you can say '*Bouchée à la reine*' when the lift's
broken and the van won't start,

If you can win and lose it all, and still be able to get to the market for
6 a.m. sharpish and greet the brand-new day with a smile and a wink,

Then the world is lovely jubbly, and everything in it,
And – more's the point – you'll be a genuine
42-carat diamond geezer,

Take it from me, my son!

FOREWORD

★★★★★★★★★★★★★★★★★★★

by Herman Aubrey Boyce

When Derek phoned to ask me to write the foreword to this, his new business guide, I had to laugh. I then checked to see if it was April 1st. I then phoned the publishers for confirmation. I then sat down and had a large brandy. Marlene (my wife) then got her oils out and offered to give me a massage. I then shot up, ran into my study, locked the door behind me and phoned Derek back just to make one final check that his first call hadn't been some kind of cruel nightmare. It hadn't been. And so here I am, self-made king of my own second-hand car empire-slash-runner-up of Shropshire's Dairy Farmer of the Year 2007–08-slash-pukka Freemason, writing the *foreword* to a *Trotter* guide to business!

What can I write about Del Boy Trotter, the 'businessman', that the press and courts of the land haven't already? A meaner critic might say that he has done for the world of business what Mike Tyson did for the world of ears. Certainly most of the items I ever bought from him either had something missing or exploded. Or both. And yet you could also say that Del and I were cut from the same cloth: we were both from humble beginnings; both students of the school of hard knocks; and we both had a burning entrepreneurial passion that refused to be extinguished. But that is where the similarities end. Without wishing to sound conceited (I can't abide snobbery), when it comes to success there really is no comparison. Of course he did eventually become a millionaire thrice over, but that was a pure fluke. Not that I wasn't pleased for him. I even managed a smile. But in the back of my mind I couldn't shake the sneaky suspicion that it wouldn't last. And sure enough, I was right.

All that said, and pushed as I am to shed a more positive light on the man who is about to 'guide' you, I do, most of the time, consider him to be a friend; he's not a grass, and he is, if nothing else, very persistent – like one of those funfair moles, you know, the ones you whack as hard as you can over and over again with a mallet but the little gits just keep on popping up for more.

Finally, a piece of advice of my own: if you should ever meet Del Boy and he asks you to go round to his for a game of poker, take a rain check.

That is all.

Boycie

INTRODUCTION

★ ★

We all have our God-given talents, don't we? Even if at first they don't seem like talents, we've all got 'em. Take my mate, Trigger, for example. From the day I first met him as a sprog it was clear that he was a couple of prawns short of a paella. Not in any dangerous way, mind you; Trig's one of my best mates and has always had a heart of gold. It just so happens that he also has the IQ of an onion bhaji. By the time we left school he didn't have a clue what he wanted to do with his life and took to just wandering the streets aimlessly, like a Mars bar wrapper in the breeze, stopping every now and then to say hello to a magpie. His hopes rose when he applied to become a Unigate milkman, but he failed the intelligence test. Next he tried to join the Flat Earth Society, but even they wouldn't have him.

Then one fateful day his Grandad Arthur introduced him to a broom. Arthur had been a road sweeper for donkey's years, and he obviously felt the time had come to pass the mantle on to Trig – either that or he just wanted to get him out of the house. According to Trigger, standing there staring at that broom, he was overcome by a warm sensation flooding his body and a strange humming in his ears. He'd discovered a sense of purpose. He'd discovered his destiny! He'd also just the day before been diagnosed with a severe case of glandular fever and was dosed up to the eyeballs, so that might have had something to do with it. But ever since that day he's been working tirelessly with that broom to keep the streets of Peckham clean(ish).

Others, like my better half, Raquel, have a flair for dramatics and singing (she's got the lungs of an angel, and that's no lie). Then there's my younger brother and business partner, Rodney, who's always enjoyed numbers and mucking about with paint, bless him. But then there are those very special and under-appreciated few who were born with a mind for business, an eye for the deal and a nose for the readies! Yes, I'm talking about the movers and the shakers of this world, the visionaries, the empire builders ... the business entrepreneur extraordinaires! And this just so happens to be the area in which I exceed. Just to be clear, though, I'm not talking about the run-of-the-mill chinless wonders you see on *The Apprentice*, I'm talking about the big-league bods: the Elton Musks, the Don Trumps,* and that sort who invented the wonder mop!

When it comes to the art of closing deals I've been around the track more times than a lurcher. Not only have I been there, done it and bought the T-shirt, I've gone back round to do it again, printed my own T-shirts, knocked 'em out at ridiculously low prices and cut the competition out of the market. In short: I taught myself to run before I could crawl and went on to ski the entrepreneurial pistes with the kind of style and grace not seen since Nijinsky took to the rink.

---

* I'm very much Peckham's answer to Trump. Not looks-wise, obviously – he's an ugly git – I just mean that not only have we both left large and remarkable stains on the world of business, we also have the same initials and we both live in towers.

Point being: in this great journey we call life, I made sure from the off that I had a front-car seat on the business roller coaster. I wanted to experience every twist and turn and every dip and peak. And I did. I went from nothing to something, back to nothing, back to a bit of something – and I still ain't given up getting back to a *full* something. And although I'm semi-retired now (my son, Damien, runs the firm these days), my mind is still as sharp as ever and the knowledge it contains is a very sought-after commodity.

So much so that I've even taken to doing a spot of consultancy work. To be honest I didn't want to, but I got fed up with the phone calls from all the big firms hungry for a slice of my precious insight. Just last week I was asked to give a motivational speech at Peckham's very own Advanced Electronics Research and Development Centre (a.k.a. Ron's Cash and Carry). I haven't said yes yet but I'll probably do it. They were raided by the Old Bill last month so they need a bit of perking up.

Anyway, I divest. This isn't really about me. This is about *you* and the golden opportunity you have right now to take a dip inside my brain and soak up some of the entrepreneurial juices that have pooled there over the years. This game we call 'business' ain't a stroll in the park. It's a rocky road full of potholes, speed cameras, people who don't indicate, mouthy cyclists and all sorts of obstacles designed to get on your tits. But fear not, as this book you're holding now is *the* definitive business guide. Packed full of insider knowledge, tips, warnings, case studies and interviews, it is designed pacifically to help steer you in the right direction – just think of it as your own personal stat-nav on the corporate highway. And whether you're just starting off or you've already got a few miles on your clock, you'll find some 42-carat gems here to help you on your way.

I can't promise it will all be plain sailing. I can't offer you any guarantees (or your money back, I'm afraid), but who knows, with a little bit of luck, a lot of savvy and a following wind, this time next year you might just end up being a millionaire!

Boeuf à la mode.
DT

Founder/CEO/President Elect
Trotters Independent Trading Co.
(1980–present)

PART ONE

★★★★★★★★★★★★★★★★

WELCOME TO THE JUNGLE

★

When I was about eight or nine my Great-Uncle George told me something that I would never ever forget. George had fought at Passchendaele during the First World War and he had one of those thousand-yard stares. He never used to say much, so when he did open his mouth it always got your attention. Anyway, one Christmas he sat me down and, fixing me with those weary eyes that had seen so much (*too much*), he told me this little parable.

'There are two types of people in this world, Del Boy,' he said. 'Wolves and sheep. And lions.'

Naturally I was all ears.

'The sheep,' he continued, 'are weak and loyal to anyone and everyone. The old wolf is cunning, but his strength is in the pack. The lion, strong all by himself, is loyal only to his pride.'

Makes sense, I thought, abnormally perceptive even back then as a sprog. My ears pricked up, eager to receive more wisdom.

'Then there's the shark,' he went on. 'The shark is strong but is loyal only to himself.'

Now I come to think about it I can't remember exactly how it went from there. He basically just listed animals for the best part of twenty minutes. (I'm sure there was a rabbit involved somewhere.) Whatever, you know what I'm getting at. George had had a skinful at the time anyway – it was Christmas. And while I never really understood the overall moral to the story, it was very impressive all the same and I like to think it helped shape the man I was to become.

Now the time has come for me to be the wise old teacher and for you to prick up *your* lugholes.* We've got a long old journey ahead of us, but don't worry. As the ancient Chinese used to say:

> ★ **IF YOU'RE GOING ON A LONG TRIP, YOU'VE GOTTA START SOMEWHERE, AIN'T YER?** ★

(Or words to that effect.)

LITTLE ACORNS

The NCP started with a bombsite. Henry Ford started with a barn. Chris Evans started with a pair of glasses and ginger hair. I started with some hooky LPs and a winning smile. Actually, it all began for me a bit earlier than that.

It's difficult to pinpoint the exact moment this gift of mine revealed itself, but it might have been during the school nativity play when I was a nipper. I was playing the role of the innkeeper, the one that told poor old Mary and Joseph to jog on when they popped in to see if he had any vacancies. I only had one line: *'There ain't no room in the inn.'* But old Joseph went in for the haggle and started asking after my stable (his missus was well and truly up the duff and about to burst, so you can't blame him really). Naturally I took the ball and started dribbling, offering him the stable at one-and-six for the night. This

---

* In case you're still a bit wet behind them (or you're from up north, Islington or somewhere like that), 'lugholes' means ears. If you find you can't understand some of the lingo in this book, there's a useful guide on page 263.

was a bit steep for Joseph so I tried to sweeten the deal by chucking in a bit of egg and bacon – Mary looked like she needed it, the poor mare. Of course none of this was in the script and the headmaster gave me a right hiding for it, but it was obvious to anyone there with half a head of sense that I was already a bit special.

My first little foray into the exciting world of the commodities market began back in the 1950s. My dad (if you can call him that), Reg, suffered terribly with a sticky mattress, and up till this point it had most of the time been down to my dear mum, Joan, to be the breadwinner of the family. My grandad, Ted, lived with us, but the only work I ever saw him manage was when he'd get up to change the channel on the telly. Apparently the last, and only, real bit of grafting he'd done was when he had a stint as a painter and decorator for the council. But that was in 1924. His main mode of transport was a horse!

It all began when I was eleven when Reg very kindly got me not one but *two* paper rounds. There I was every morning, come rain, sleet or shine: thirty-five *Daily Sketches*, forty *Heralds* and a *Spick and Span* for the weirdo in Marley Road. And when I finished that route I went to another shop to start my second round. I didn't even have a bike.

On the upside it did teach me a lot about responsibility and the value of money. More importantly it allowed me to get to know the locals, do a bit of market research and build up my very own little clientele. This was back during the glory days of the black market; rationing had not long since ended and luxury consumer goods that people had only ever dreamed about were becoming more widely available. At the time Reg had done the unthinkable, peeled himself off his mattress and got himself some part-time work down at the docks, meaning he could, and did, get his hands on all sorts of high-quality and exotic merchandise. He supplied the gear, I knocked it out on my rounds and we divvied up the profits. In the end I was making so much on my paper rounds that I didn't need the papers no more. Of course, I'm not recommending you do anything like this. To modern ears it all sounds a bit naughty, but they were different times back then.

I also kept myself busy down the markets, nothing big to begin with, just watching how it all worked and pitching in where and when I could. It helped Mum, put Reg's back up, and left me with a few bob for myself, so it was very much a win-win-win situation. I had to step up my game a bit though when Rodney was born – *thirteen* bleedin', years after me! – what with having another mouth to feed. And stone me, he went through rusks like nobody's business! A few years later, when we lost Mum (she died), Reg, true to form, packed his bags and had it away on his toes. So there I was, little more than a boy and now the man of the house. Those were some rough days and on more than one occasion I came close to derailing, but that's another story altogether.

★ **START LOCAL, THINK GLOBAL.
FROM BUCHAREST TO HULL, US TROTTERS HAVE
BEEN A MAJOR PLAYER ON THE WORLD STAGE.** ★

To this day people still talk about our homemade fish fingers.
Eels on Wheels, circa 1967, before the health inspector stuck the kibosh on it.

FISHY BUSINESS

My first big break came in 1967 when I went into partnership with a mate of mine, Jumbo Mills. You see, he knew this geezer, John-Boy, who worked a cushty little number at a Mac Fisheries. Now, John-Boy had let it be known that he weren't against doing a bit of business 'off the clock', i.e. he could get his hands on a regular supply of dirt-cheap reject fish. I say reject (that's what was written on the crates) but you never would have known. And according to John-Boy they weren't rejected 'cos they weren't fresh, it was 'cos the regulation bods upstairs had stamped them too unattractive for the shop floor. I remember at the time this striking me as odd. I don't know about you but I've never once clocked an attractive haddock (you're gonna eat the sodding thing, not take it to the pictures!). Anyway, John-Boy had it all: cod, plaice, cockles, whelks … Well, it didn't take an Alec Sugar to know that we were on to a winner!

★ **GIVE A MAN A FISH AND HE'LL EAT FOR A DAY. GIVE HIM A REGULAR SUPPLY OF DIRT-CHEAP FISH IN AN OLD HANDCART AND HE'LL MAKE A NICE BIT OF BUNSE!** ★

And that's how Eels on Wheels was born. I was the front man, of course; I couldn't stomach getting wrist deep in all those guts and fluids like Jumbo could. And for a while we were making a tidy little profit. The only downside was the smell. I got through at least a bottle of Brut a day trying to cover it up. Jumbo didn't seem to mind, but then he never smelled too clever in the first place. Of course the dream couldn't last and people started to get jealous of our success. That's when the rumours of a food poisoning epidemic began to spread, and before you knew it the health inspector stuck the kibosh on us. Eels on Wheels had flogged its final winkle. It was a sad day, but it had been an education. The biggest lesson it taught me was that I belonged up front in the thick of the action, dealing with the customers one to one. Only next time I'd be doing it without smelling like a sardine's armpit.

BRANCHING OUT

After the wheels came off Eels on Wheels, I did a bit of work on the John Player Special circuit – delivering fags round Lewisham. I was earning but there was no challenge in it and I missed the interaction with the public, so next I decided to branch out a bit further afield and ended up doing the old Happy Snaps at the Tower of London (second-hand Brownie, no film, pound a go – lovely jubbly!). It was the perfect opportunity for me to brush up on my people skills. Not that I needed it really. You see, I've always been at ease around people, and, more importantly, I've always had a natural gift for putting people at ease. It don't matter where I am or who I'm with; I could be down the Crown and Anchor enjoying a pint of bitter and a pickled onion with the market boys, or having a chinwag over a plate of swan and peas in the banquet hall of one of England's finest stately homes – people just seem to relax around me.

Of course, I also had Rodney to look after, and I did everything I could to make him feel normal. Trust me, that weren't easy. Once he'd grown up (and I mean *grown* in the strictest sense of the word – there were giraffes on steroids that couldn't keep up with him!), it was time to bring him into the fold. He'd finished school and, with my help, had bagged himself a couple of GCEs, one in maths, one in art. *Now there's some talent that can be put to good use*, I thought to myself. *But how?* That was 1974 and I'm still struggling with the answer to this day. He was reluctant at first, declaring his need for independence to any poor sod who'd listen, but then he got in a spot of bother with the Old Bill and before you could shout '*drugs squad!*' he was rushing back to the shelter of his big brother's wing. Actually, I quite liked having him back, even though I wouldn't tell him that. He weren't a

With my business acumen, energy, drive and unbreakable will to succeed – and Rodney's two GCEs – there was no stopping us.

danger to nobody; he was just going through that awkward phase, a bit like a trifle, you know, thick and fruity. He obviously just needed some guidance, that's all.

Come the beginning of the 1980s, change was in the air. The time had arrived for the Trotters to face the brave new world as a proper, McCoy, company. You see, I had this dream. In it, Rodney and me owned a skyscraper office block on the South Bank. We were standing on the balcony of the penthouse suite with a couple of sorts, Gabrielle and Bianca, bra-less, but with class. We were sipping red drinks and conversing over a liver-sausage sandwich and a vol-au-vent or two, and above us, on top of this skyscraper, in fifty-foot-high neon lettering, were the initials of 'Trotters Independent Traders'!

Trotters Independent Trading's official logo.

Sends a little tingle down your spine, don't it?

THE GOODS

Now, let's skip forward a decade or two and allow me to take you on a journey through my warehouse/garage – or as I like to think of it: the dream centre.

- On your right: one mint condition prophetic leg.

- On your left: two DIY gas conversion kits, circa 1969.

- Over here: a crate of Showaddywaddy LPs, not a scratch on 'em.

- Over there: a set of windscreen wipers for a Citroën Berlingo.

- Delving deeper, you'll notice up on the shelf there: five fractionally warped Rubik's cubes.

- And over the back, behind the louvre door: an air filter for a nuclear fallout shelter.

Some people (Rodney) might call it a load of old rubbish, but it's my bread and butter (and the little git never complained when he was scoffing it down his gullet!). You'll notice a good mix of gear here with no common theme. You'd be right. And wrong. You see, I'm a general trader with an eye for the unique item. But then I cater to the paying punter and I've always relished a challenge.

You'd be surprised what people are willing to part with their hard-earned cash for. Example: you might not fancy sitting down at Christmas and tucking into a one-legged turkey, but others might not be that fussed. Look at the positives. At the end of the day a turkey's a turkey, however many legs it's got, breast is best anyway, and at the very least it'll give you all something to talk about round the dinner table.

Where dreams are made.

RECOGNISING QUALITY

Stumpy turkeys aside, it's the rare and specialist item that I'm a sucker for. When it comes to spotting a diamond in the rough, I never switch off, and I suggest you don't either. Like the gold prospectors of old, sifting through the dirt for a glimmering nugget, keep your mince pies peeled for the gems, because as I of all people know, they *are* out there.

As luck would have it, I've always been a bit of a culture vulture. Oh yes, there really is nothing like a bit of art to nourish the soul. From the Renaissance daubers like Van Coff right on through to Indian

In safe hands. Me picking up another bargain of a lifetime, circa 1983.

sculpture greats like Ming (he made some wonderful stuff, pity he had to go and die when he did), my eye is finely tuned for a quality piece. And it's just as well really, 'cos over the years Trotters Independent Traders has found itself on more than one occasion having a dabble in the world of antiques and fine *object-dart*. Gothic classics, Art Dicko, modern collectables, I have a natural instinct for the history and value of a piece. And while there have been times when I've needed to consult an expert, I much prefer to go with my gut (in my experience most of these so-called 'experts' wouldn't know a Royal Doulton if it jumped up and jabbed 'em in the Jacobs).

My main areas of expertise (or my *raison fruit de mer*, as the French would say) are furniture and timepieces – Queen Anne cabinets, Georgian digital clocks, that sort of thing – but I've never let that restrict me. Over the years I've knocked out everything from a fully ergonomic Baroque executive swivel-chair to an original eighteenth-century Barbie doll (minus the original packaging, of course). But that's not to say that I don't sometimes make the wrong call – I once discovered what I thought was a genuine Elizabethan hot-water bottle at a car boot sale. Turned out it was from Superdrug.

TOP TIP!

★

BRUSH UP YOUR KNOWLEDGE BY WHACKING THE ANTIQUES ROADSHOW ON THE OLD SKY PLUS. I'VE WRITTEN TO THE SHOW SEVERAL TIMES OVER THE YEARS REGARDING A CHIPPENDALE TEAPOT, BUT IT STILL AIN'T GOT ROUND TO PECKHAM.

★

OPERATIONS HQ

Being a born-and-bred Peckhamite, Peckham, south London, has always been my main trading floor. But when I'm not out having a mosey and seeing what business I can drum up in the pubs and auction houses, I do most of my work from Trotter Headquarters: Flat 127, Nelson Mandela House (known locally, and with affection, as Trotter Tower). It also seconds as my home, which comes in handy when I fancy a quick power-nap as the bed is right on hand. Not that I kip that much. People like me have got too much going on for sleep.

I've always found that being up high makes me think more clearly. There's just something about being up above the rat race in your own little castle in the clouds that does that. It has its downsides, of course, but if you can zone out the occasional pigeon slamming into the balcony, the rumble of low-flying jumbo jets, Raquel's Hoover and the biannual riots down in the precinct, it really is very peaceful.

More importantly, this is where the cogs of the business turn and the major executive decisions are made. When I'm not pacing the floor on the old dog and bone, adding the final touches to deals in the kind of far-away lands you only ever heard of in *Whicker's World* (Formosa, Walsall, Bok Choy etc), I'll be in the conference room (kitchen) having a heated debate with Rodney about the pros and cons of investing in olive oil. If I'm not there, I'll be at my desk (dining table) catching up with my correspondence or banging out a belligerent memo. Sometimes I like to conduct a little R&D (Research and Development) on my way to and from the rubbish chute. It's a tightly wound, fast-paced operation, and I wouldn't have it any other way.

Peckham's answer to the Gherkin.

PART TWO

★★★★★★★★★★★★★★★★

BEING THE BOSS

★

Like it or not, a natural food chain exists in most office environments. The technical term for this is 'office hierarchy'. It makes sense really. Study the average gang of gorillas (I haven't, but it's on my bucket list) and you'll more than likely find an old and knackered one who's seen it all and now just wants nothing more than to sit about picking ticks off himself (Grandad). You'll also find the young upstart, the sort who beats his chest and gives it all the big' un in front of the lady gorillas but at the end of the day can't cut the mustard and skulks off to his bedroom to pout and watch *Home and Away* (Rodney). But then you'll find the silverback, alpha-male gorilla, the one who swings from the highest trees and brings home the biggest bananas, you know, the good-looking and debonair one that all the other gorillas turn to when the tom-tit hits the fan (yours truly).

WHICH ONE ARE YOU?

Of course this can all lead to some heated territorial disputes, so expect the occasional banging of heads and throwing of dung. This was very true of Rodney as a young man, who, for some reason, took a lot longer than most to grow out of the 'idealist student' phase. (Oh yes, he loved a protest. One time he even went on a politically motivated hunger strike. It lasted one and an 'alf days before he sent out for a curry. But that was Rodney, a textbook case of a rebel-without-balls if ever there was one.)

It was also particularly problematic during the mating season when he'd get a sudden rush of testosterone to his brain. And just as the rutting stag grunts and stomps the floor when he fancies a bit, Rodney, too, gave off his own unique warning signs – his eyes would go all goggly and he'd start doing a funny walk (think John Wayne with a jockstrap full of itching powder). I dunno, I sometimes think he learned the art of seduction watching *Wildlife on One*. Not that it ever fazed me. Normally a stern look was enough to readdress the natural order.

★ **WITH GREAT POWER COMES GREAT RESPONSIBILITY.**
SPIDER-MAN'S UNCLE ★

Bottom line: everyone dreams of being the boss (their own and/or someone else's). But I'm here now to tell you it ain't a bed of roses. Part of being the *nouveau uno* (or *Capo Del Monte,* as they say in the Basque region) is wielding the power to tell people what to do: ordering them about, disciplining them, and even having to *fire* them if necessary. But like I said, it also has its downsides. People rely on you and if things go pear-shaped the buck stops firmly at your door – and sometimes, as I so often and painfully discovered, no amount of blaming a Rodney will wash. And that's why, if you one day find yourself in the position of being the big cheese among the Mini Cheddars, it's important to be the best one you can be.

South London's answer to the Rockefellers – the Trotters of Peckham.

Being a good boss doesn't just take wisdom, hard work, drive, energy and an unbreakable desire to succeed. It also requires emotional intelligence, sensitivity and tact. Remember, you're not just responsible for the firm and its success, you're also responsible for your employees and their emotional development. It never hurts to bear in mind that they don't just see you as their boss, they look up to you as a role model, a mentor, a guiding light in a world filled with all too much darkness, if you like. So you should always take time every now and then to check in on them and find out what's happening in their lives. If, like Rodney, they tell you to mind your own bloody business, at least keep an eye out for the little signs that something's wrong.

FINANCIAL MANAGEMENT AND LAW

Back in 1980, not long after the birth of Trotters Independent Traders, I made two major decisions. They were dark days in general back then as the country was still in the grip of recession and some three million were unemployed. Rodney (or 'Peckham's Conscience' as he's been known) felt this discontent very deeply and aired it often. To help take his mind off things I decided it was time he faced a new challenge and made him a full partner in the firm. When that didn't work I promoted him to the position of Financial Adviser – a risky move, but what with the GCE in maths and his love of titles, I thought it would at the very least shut him up for a while.

Of course, I ended up regretting it. Don't get me wrong, the boy knew his way round a calculator, but I didn't realise just how seriously he'd take to his new role. You see, when I told him he could handle the company accounts, I didn't think he'd actually start taking accounts! Before I knew what was happening he was knocking out spreadsheets all over the shop! It was messing my system up. I always preferred a 'less-paperwork-the-better' approach to this sort of thing, and when it came to cash flow my only concern was that I had enough on the hip to cover my overheads and keep the bailiffs from the door. And just as I've never needed a weatherman to tell me that it's pissing down, I've never needed a piece of paper to tell me my pockets are empty!

On top of that there was always the chance this paperwork might fall into the 'wrong' hands. Some might call this unprofessional, or even bordering on the dodgy, but I called it being a pragmatist. All right, we might not have been paying VAT, income tax or National Insurance, but on the other hand we weren't claiming dole money, social security or supplementary benefits – the government didn't give us nothing so

Grandad. About as useful as a pair of sunglasses on a bloke with one ear. I miss him every day.

we didn't give the government nothing. Couldn't say fairer than that, could I?*All that said, you'd be hard pushed to find anyone more respectful of the law than me. Without it this delicate house of cards we call society would implode quicker than one of Grandad's Christmas puddings.

Of course, you could also play devil's advocado and argue a completely different case. It was, after all, the great Charles Dickens who wrote, '*The law is a right pain in the arse!*' (or something *very* similar). I'm not saying he was right, but I can see what he was getting at.

---

* Of course nowadays I make sure that everything is done strictly above board. I've got receipts up to my eyeballs and me and the Inland Revenue get on like a house on fire. A smashing bunch of lads!

COMPANY POLICY

Every company sets its own rules of conduct and conditions of employment: dress code, attendance and termination policies,* all that gubbins. My own personal approach to this has always been pretty laid-back – as I said, it cuts down on the paperwork. No red tape or small print involved; as long as you agree not to take liberties, a nod and a firm handshake is as good as a signature in my book.

That said, if you work for me you can count some rules as given. For example, my door is always open. I only ask that you knock before entering, just in case I'm in my pants. I also have a pretty strict rule when it comes to smoking and try to make sure the flat is well stocked up at all times with cigars, lighters and ashtrays. But one thing you can never be too complacent about is your policy on substance abuse, and I speak from experience here. In his younger days, Rodney was known to enjoy the occasional pinch of Rastafarian Old-Holborn. He weren't an addict or nothing like that, it was more of a recreational habit brought on by a host of underlying factors: a need for escapism, a desire to fit in and look 'cool', a chance to expand his artistic horizons, and just an all-round general wallyishness.

TOP TIP!

★

KEEP YOUR EYES PEELED FOR THE FUNNY FAGS.

★

---

* I never had to worry about this. Rodney self-terminated on a regular basis. I basically had to rehire him about once a fortnight.

HEALTH AND SAFETY

Being the guv'nor of your very own pukka company means that not only are you responsible for maintaining a safe and non-toxic work environment, but also for making sure that your staff receive the very best of care and attention when accidents and illness happen. Having strict health and safety procedures in place is a must for any self-respecting firm, and Trotters Independent Traders is no different.

Having raised Rodney since he was five years old, it's no wonder I'm a dab hand at dealing with ailments. He was one of those sprogs that was frequently under the weather, with viruses, fungal infections, belly ache, measles (German and regular British ones), chicken pox, colds, flus and anaemia. Nothing got past that boy. One week he'd have the two-bob-bits, the next he'd be egg-bound. Stone me, hardly a month went by when he didn't have a runny nose or a manky eye. He was like a Center Parcs for germs!

'*But what do I do in an emergency?!*' I hear you cry.

First things first, don't panic. Calmly assess the situation, put pressure on any open wounds and call for an ambulance. While you're waiting (traffic can be murder), have a rummage through your first aid kit. Ours is under the sink. Now, what you put in your kit is entirely up to you. Feel free to consult a qualified medical specialist, but a regular stock of the following has always seen me right:

- Plasters
- Savlon
- TCP
- Bonjela

- Immodium Instant
- Vicks VapoRub
- Bloke-sized Kleenex
- Baileys and orangeade (to settle an upset tummy)

But it all depends really on the level of emergency. It might just be a simple dose of the squits or a door slammed on a finger. Or it might be something a bit more serious …

CASE STUDY #01

Back during the long hot summer of 1976, Rodney came home from the park one day suffering a serious bout of sunstroke. I knew something was up the minute he crawled in the front room. He had this strange glow about him. At first I thought he'd just overdone it with the Ready Brek (he always loved his oats) but then I felt his forehead. It was so hot you could've fried an egg on it.

Immediately realising that time was of the essence, I took control of the situation by slinging him over my shoulder, chucking him in a freezing-cold bath and whacking a bag of ice cubes on his mooey. An hour later he did a full circle and went into what Dr Becker (the family GP) called 'hypothermic shock'. Realising, once again, that time was of the essence, I dragged him out of the bath and slung him in the airing cupboard to defrost. Four hours later he was right as rain.

All in all it was a very traumatic lesson in the importance of sunscreen, and from that day forward I always made sure to put a bottle of Ambre Solaire in his lunchbox.

A Health and Safety nightmare, especially during the mating season.
Rodders, circa 1982.

CASE STUDY #02

On another occasion, Rodney accidentally swallowed a two-pence piece. Grandad and I were watching a particularly interesting episode of *Kojak* at the time and so we didn't actually see him do it, but when he staggered over clutching his throat and gasping for air, I could tell something weren't right. 'What's wrong, Rodders?' I asked, 'Your Hobson's playing up?' He didn't answer, naturally, and instead fell to his knees.

'He don't look well, does he, Del?' Grandad chipped in. And he didn't. He looked bloody 'orrible. It was then I noticed his lips were blue. 'He's been at those Slush Puppies again,' I said. 'I warned him not to have too many.'

A few moments later, as his eyeballs rolled into the back of his head, the terrifying truth dawned on me. Quick as a flash I hoisted him up and flipped him upside down. This was not as easy as it sounds as he was seventeen at the time and already well over six foot. I'll never forget the way he thrashed and squirmed, his plimsolls kicking me in the chin as I slammed him up and down, up and down, over and over. It was after about the tenth slam, to my huge relief, that the coin shot out. Unfortunately he'd only half an hour earlier polished off an entire Emperor burger and chips, so, as you can imagine, it weren't the only thing that shot out. I never liked that rug anyway.

Bottom line: Be it a paper-cut or a peanut stuck up a nostril, even the most cosiest and innoculous-looking work space is fraught with hidden peril. Keep on your toes and be ready to act.

JOB SATISFACTION

If your team ain't happy, the whole business suffers. This was a recurring problem I had with Rodney, but it weren't for the want of trying. From day one I did everything I could to make it interesting for him, and over the years he took on many different and desirable roles within the firm: Financial Adviser/Accountant; Director of Sales; Director of Commercial Development; Road Manager; Nocturnal Security Officer; Chief Dog Sitter; Car Cleaner ... Come to think of it there ain't much he hasn't been.

But was he grateful for the wealth of variety and experience that his big brother so thoughtfully put his way? No, he weren't. And keep in mind here that he didn't have it too bad. He got a day off every year on his birthday, free training, a company vehicle, maternity leave! And he didn't have to worry about incurring any travel expenses; he lived here! Most people would rip your arm off for that sort of package.

One of his biggest faults was his untrusting nature. For some reason he always had it in his head that he was getting a raw deal and that I was cheating him in some way. I lost count of the times I had to say to him, 'Come on, Rodney, it's everything between you and me split straight down the middle, sixty-forty.' Being the firm's accountant you'd have thought he'd have already known this, the wally! I had been hoping the situation would improve as he got older, but if anything he got worse.

Not that I didn't sympathise with him. Stress played a major role (see page 206). It reached the point where I felt so bad seeing him under so much pressure that I decided to place an ad in the *Peckham Echo* looking to hire someone to help take the load off his shoulders.

*I remember this one being taken. I'd just promised Rodney
a year's subscription to Penthouse.*

I got one application … *from Rodney!* The saucy git was looking for another job behind my back!

From a managerial point of view, job dissatisfaction may at first glance just seem like ingratitude or laziness, but it should be taken seriously. Left unchecked it will only get worse and that kind of low morale can be contagious – one week your finance department is in a mope, the next your marketing team are kipping on the job. Before you know it your entire staff is calling in sick. It's like the corporate world's equivalent of haemorrhoids. What starts off as a minor discomfort ends in keyhole surgery and a fortnight of hobbling around like you've got rickets.

Watch your team carefully and be aware of the subtle little signs:

- Irritability
- Low productibility
- Lack of concentration
- Yawning
- Psoriasis
- Alopecia
- Crying
- Muttering, 'I'm gonna kill you, I'm gonna kill you, *I am*, I'm gonna kill you!' over and over again.

> ★ **DON'T FALL VICTIM TO CORPORATE PILES. NIP IT IN THE BUD ASAP (AS SHARPISH AS POSSIBLE).** ★

MOTIVATION

One of the best ways to fend off job dissatisfaction is to keep your staff hungry. No, I don't mean ban lunch; I'm talking about motivation. And one of the best ways to motivate is to lead by example. Like the general heading the gallant charge across no-man's land, what better way to inspire others to follow than by sticking your own neck on the line? And that's why there is nothing I ever asked Rodney to do that I wouldn't, and didn't, do myself. I can't think of a pacific example right now off the top of my head, but there must have been loads.

Another good way to keep your team engaged and ensure loyalty is to put some time aside every now and then to bond with them. All the big firms do it nowadays – you know, those morale-building outings where you learn to trust each other, group hug and all that cobblers. Ahead of my time, as usual, I was already doing this way back when. Every day without fail us Trotters would end up in our local, the Nag's Head, for a few liveners. Granted, there weren't much hugging involved, and very little trust either, but I usually felt a bit better afterwards.

Here're some other ways to keep your team firing on all four cylinders:

⮕ INCENTIVE GIFTS

Every year I'd get Rodney the latest Bic (he always loved a Biro), but for special occasions it doesn't hurt to push the boat out a bit. I once got Rodney a chunky gold identity bracelet engraved with his name.

He was gobsmacked when he saw it. In fact, so taken aback was he with this thoughtful gesture that he actually had tears in his eyes when he put it on. He was even more emotional when, two weeks later, his arm started to turn green. I dunno, some people just can't handle the purity of the carats.

⮞ WORDS

Words can have a big impact on morale, so choose them carefully. Use a combination of direct, powerful and uplifting words. For example, rather than just saying 'Hurry up!', I've always found that 'Get a move on you dipstick!' or 'Put your back into it you lazy git!' are much more effective. Another good one is: 'Oi, come on you dozy twonk, these crates ain't gonna shift themselves!' Mix it up a bit and be creative.

⮞ KEEP 'EM ON THEIR TOES

If you want to run a tight ship, you have to constantly train and test your crew. I once got Rodney to lug a load of boxes down the stairs and put them into the van. No sooner had he done that, I then got him to unload them and take them back up to the flat. I then explained to him that I didn't actually need the boxes moved, I just wanted to see how long it would take him to do it. He didn't talk to me for three months and I had to win him back with a new pair of Doc Martens and a Betamax copy of *Debbie Does Dallas*. Was it worth it? Yes. Yes it was.

➲ INVOLVEMENT

Include others in your brainstorming sessions (or '*thought showers*' as the whizz kids like to call them). I even went so far as to get Trigger involved once. I was desperate for a new angle when I hit upon the idea of inventions. There's a lot of dough to be made in that game if you get it right. I mean, look at that bloke who invented the Dyson vacuum cleaner. I forget his name now but he ain't short of a few bob, that's for sure. Always one to think outside the box, Trigger blew Rodney and me away by not only coming up with an idea but also designing a prototype. Fair enough, it was a foldable backscratcher made out of two chopsticks (which also came in handy when you wanted to point at things), but you couldn't fault him for effort.

➲ COMPANY FUNCTIONS

Chuck a good Christmas do. No need to get fancy. A few swift halves at your local followed by a festive Ruby Murray should do the trick.

➲ IF ALL ELSE FAILS ...

A smidge of emotional blackmail can work wonders.

★ **TRUST + MOTIVATION + EMOTIONAL BLACKMAIL = A HAPPY AND PRODUCTIVE TEAM!** ★

DELEGATING

As much as it would be nice to do everything yourself, sometimes it just ain't possible. And that's when you've got to hand responsibility over to someone on your team. And it can't be just any old person, it has to be someone you trust, someone you know will take to the challenge with the personal care, diligence and pride that it deserves. Of course in my case Rodney *was* my team, so I was well and truly lumbered.

> ★ **'SEND RODNEY FOR THE FISH.'**
> MUM, ON HER DEATHBED ★

You'd have thought he'd have jumped at these opportunities to prove himself capable, but most of the time he just moaned that I was distracting him from more important things, like *Top of the Pops* or the latest issue of *Readers' Wives*. Occasionally, though, when the job demanded it, I'd also have to get Grandad or my Great-Uncle Albert on board, but as I very quickly discovered, asking them not to nause a job up was like asking a Labrador not to shit on your lawn.

But then there were times when the job required *specialist* care and attention …

CASE STUDY #03

Back in the early nineties I found myself having to get shot of two dozen drums of chemical waste from Grandad's allotment. We'd long since lost Grandad (he died) by this point and I'd forgotten we even had an allotment.

That was until the council wrote to warn us that for the last decade or so it had been used as a dumping ground and was now posing an environmental hazard. Well, being the ecologically aware bloke that I am (see page 228), I was just as concerned as they were when I saw those dirty old drums all over the place. Realising the danger, I immediately sought expert advice. Trigger, who the council had just

Striving for a non-toxic work environment.
Albert, me and Rodney on Grandad's allotment, circa 1992.

promoted to the position of 'Environmental Hygienist', opened up a drum and had a peek inside.

'It's some sort of yellow stuff,' he said. Not quite the detailed report I was after, but you couldn't really argue with the diagnosis. Whatever it was, it weren't good. Rodney suggested it might even have been toxic.

'It could be bloody poisonous an' all!' I said.

I had to get rid of it quick. Trigger said we could drop it off at a 24-hour waste-disposal depot he used to work at. Rodney, being his usual helpful self, didn't fancy the job, so I then had to get my old mate Denzil on board. He's a smashing bloke, Denzil, very trusting and loyal, plus he had an empty van. Of course he chucked his penny's worth in on the contents of the drums (everything from 'killer gunge' to Concorde fuel!). After some initial effin' and blindin', my hastily formed A-team loaded the drums into the van and off we went to the 24-hour waste-processing plant. It was closed.

'Well, it is a bit late,' Trigger said.

'You said it was open twenty-four hours a day,' I reminded him.

'Yeah, but not at night.'

By this point my arse was starting to get an 'eadache, so I decided to leave the job to Trigger and Denzil. Not that I was being flippant about the whole matter. The welfare of the planet is right up there on my list of priorities. I can't tell you how many bouts of acid reflux I've had over the old global warming crisis and all that game. But I was paying 'em fifty quid each for their efforts and I had complete faith in whatever their final decision would be. And, as I later explained to the magistrate, the fact that they ended up dumping the drums in a local pond was as much a shock to me as it was to everyone else.

PART THREE

★★★★★★★★★★★★★★★★★★

IMAGE

★

As Jesus said to Moses at the Sermon on the Mount: 'Clothes maketh the man.' And how very right he was …

Like it or not, first impressions count and if you want to be taken seriously in this game, you've gotta look the part. Trust me, go that extra mile in the way you present yourself and the returns will be tenfold. This is something I always tried to impress on Rodney. You see, when you step out onto that trading room floor, you're not just selling your wares, you're selling *yourself*. To be fair though, in Rodney's case it weren't so much that he needed to get an image, it was more that he needed to get *rid* of one. All right, he could scrub up smart when pushed, but most of the time he went about looking like a cross between Swampy and a Boomtown Rat.

'But I can't afford all that fancy designer gear, Del!' I hear you say. Don't worry, neither can most of the yuppies who wear it – they're just living in sin with their flexible friends. Remember, I'm only talking *appearances* here, and the right appearance can fool the customer. It's all about the subtle art of suggestion, the aim being to leave people in no doubt whatsoever as to the sort of person you are.

CLOBBER

Wear a suit. Go for a silk shirt (or something that passes as silk – my mate Monkey Harris is the man to talk to on this), pinstripe, matching breast-pocket handkerchief, brogues (I prefer Goochi) and an overcoat (camel hair's making a comeback). For a more informal look try a trendy trench coat (green is my favourite).

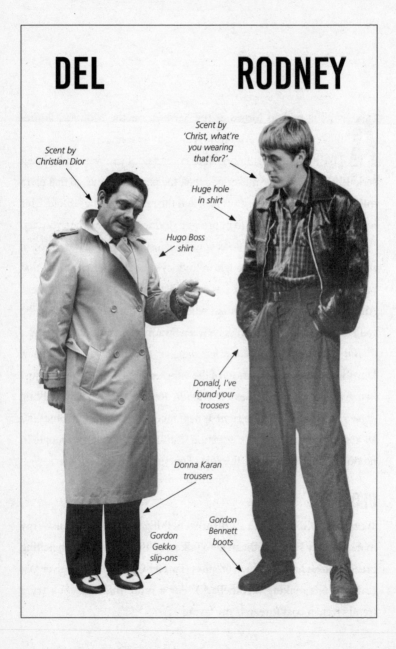

➲ ACCESSORIES

Now to add a few finishing touches:

- The aluminium briefcase/Filofax one-two is always a winning combo.

- Don a pair of *Top Gun*-style, aviation sunglasses. You can't go wrong with Roy-Ban.

- Use a money clip instead of a wallet. Don't be afraid to flash your wad.

- There's nothing cool about smoking, but if you can't resist the occasional fag, use a holder. Mine is genuine faux tortoiseshell.

- Another surefire way to dazzle is to wear a bit of gold. Nothing too flash, just enough to catch the eye: a medallion (worn outside of shirt), a sovereign ring or two, a chunky identity bracelet and a set of cufflinks (preferably personalised). It makes people think, *'Hang about, this bloke's doing all right for himself. I bet he knows a Footsy one hundred when he sees one!'*

- A quality timepiece is a must. Back in the day I opted for a gold-plated, digital watch/calculator with integrated stopwatch and reading light. It was like having Batman's utility belt on your wrist. These days a Rolox does me just fine.

- Don't forget about your reading material. There's no point in looking as though you're off to the City for a quick power-lunch with Karren Brady if you've got a rolled-up copy of *Nuts* under your arm. I always try to carry an emergency *Financial Times* (inside my aluminium briefcase) just in case.

➲ AND FOR THE LADIES …

- A well-fitted power-suit over a white blouse is a classic IMHO (in my human opinion). And by 'suit' I don't necessarily mean trousers. Not that I've got anything against women in trousers, but the whole point is that you want to make a positive impact; you don't want to frighten people. Bottom line: don't be afraid to show a bit of calf.

- Go for a pair of heels, black, not too short and not too high – aim for the 4 to 6 inches mark and you'll be laughing.

- One coat of make-up, lightly applied. You want something that lets the world know that you're a stylish sort; you don't want people mistaking you for Krusty the Clown.

- All in all you want a look that says, '*Yes, I'm a woman, but I know my onions and my balls are as big, if not bigger, than yours. Deal with it!*' But in a delightful, classy and non-threatening way.

Taking power-dressing to a whole new level. Marlene Boyce.

WARNING!

A few years back, Rodney turned up for work sporting a turquoise handbag. To be more precise, and as he insisted, it was a man's designer 'tote' bag (a present from the missus). As you can imagine, Damien and I were in fits of laughter, but as soon as I was able to talk again, I very delicately and tactfully explained to Rodney that he looked like a right fanny and that there was no way I was gonna be seen out with him and his tote. Don't get me wrong, I'm all for making a fashion statement – and, whilst I'm certainly no Eddie Lizzard, I have a couple of times come very close to connecting with my feminine side – but a line has to be drawn somewhere. Call me old-fashioned, but the only types of hold-alls a man should be seen with are sacks, wheelbarrows, executive briefcases and the occasional genuine leather-effect flight-bag.

BODY LANGUAGE

Sometimes it's better to let the walking do the talking, and this is vital in the world of business. When I enter a room I make sure I've spoken volumes before I've even opened my mouth. It's all about the stance: chin up, shoulders back, looking the world in the eye. Self-assured, tough yet graceful, it's more of a glide than a walk. When people see this, they don't just see the confident strut of the good-looking bloke about town, own teeth and all that game, they see class and sophistication. *'Now there's a man who knows the difference between a bottle of Tittinger and a can of Tango,'* they think to themselves. And that's because in their subconscious mind what they're actually

The wheat amongst the chaff. Me with Rodney and Mickey Pearce, circa 1983.

seeing is a white yacht floating on the blue waters of a Caribbean bay. More often than not with Rodney they saw a winkle barge sinking off the end of Southend Pier.

> ★ **THE NEXT TIME YOU ENTER AN IMPORTANT CONFERENCE, WALK IN LIKE YOU MEAN BUSINESS. DON'T WALK IN LIKE YOUR GUTS ARE PLAYING UP.** ★

PEN AND INK

Have you ever noticed how nothing sparks a memory quite like a sudden and strong whiff? I have. And Nelson Mandela House is full of 'em. The pong of Grandad's Christmas dinners still linger to this day, a trace of roast spuds (or lumps of anthracite, as Rodney used to call them) embedded in the kitchen lino like some sort of musty spectre. Then there's Uncle Albert's pipe, the sweet and sickly stench of which is still trapped inside the spare bedroom mattress. But there are nice smells too. Raquel, for the most part (see page 213), has always been very easy on the nose, and so has yours truly. Oh yes, say what you like about Derek Trotter, but you can't say he ain't clean. A daily shower and a splash of cologne – neck, chest, pits – lovely jubbly! That's my motto. I don't get fancy, preferring to rely mostly on dependable staples of scent like Brut, Old Spice and the odd dab of Blue Stratos.

> ★ **REMEMBER: IT DON'T MATTER HOW GOOD YOU ARE, NOBODY WANTS TO DO BUSINESS WITH SOMEONE WHO SMELLS LIKE A BIG MAC.** ★

Incidentally: a few years back Trotters Independent Traders was all set to enter the heady and fiercely competitive market of fragrance when I hit upon the idea of producing and bottling my very own personal scent. Well, if it's good enough for David Beckham, it's good enough for Derek Trotter. My aim was to capture the smell of danger mixed with a subtle hint of mint, undertones of animal magnetism and the merest suggestion of satsuma. It was no cowboy job either – I'm not one of those shysters you see down the market flogging bottles of 'Yves Saint Dior'. No, Damien took to the Google and did a full hour an half of research before we even considered commencing. Another full forty-five minutes later and we had the formula down to a fine T.

Sadly the whole project never got past the prototype stage. You see, I gave out a free bottle each to Denzil, Trigger and Rodney's old mate, Mickey Pearce, and told them to use it every day for a fortnight then give me some feedback. And whilst the actual scent of *ALPHA: The Smell of Del* received mixed reviews (ranging from 'Not the worst thing I've smelled' to 'It made me gag'), the list of unforeseen side effects did put somewhat of a downer on the entire venture. I won't go into too much detail, suffice to say it included peeling skin, itchy eyes, second-degree burns and, in Mickey's case, cheilitis (which it turns out is the technical term for chronic swelling of the lips). According to the doctor that examined him, Mickey was suffering from an allergic reaction to something known as 'potassium persulfate'.* I was gutted, but it weren't my fault. I later discovered that Damien, my chief mixologist, had accidentally added in a few glugs from a bottle of Grandad's Denta-Sheen, which he found at the back of the garage.

Needless to say it was all very upsetting and I decided there and then to leave the art of fragrance to the Kelvin Klein's and Cocoa Channels of this world.

---

* I could have sworn a lawsuit was coming on but as luck would have it Mickey got quite a few compliments on his new look and ended up coming back for two more bottles.

WHEELS

Just as what you wear, what you read, how you move and how you smell makes an immediate and lasting impact, what you drive also says a lot about the sort of person you are. Turn up for your next board meeting in the right motor and you're halfway to being home and dry.

My main set of wheels over the years has been a Reliant Regal van: yellow, two seats, three wheels, a real one of a kind. Many people have asked what drove an ostentatious, refined and switched-on bloke like me to choose a yellow three-wheel van. Most assume that it was a mere impulse buy or that I won (or lost) a bet. The truth is a lot of careful and multi-layered thought went into the acquisition. But the space in the back and other practicalities aside, the main deciding factor was the colour. That's right. I've always been a big believer in colour psychology and how different colours promote different emotions.

First off, and from a marketing perspective, yellow is the brightest colour on the plectrum and therefore the most noticeable to the human eye. It's also the colour of optimism and creativity – both core attributes of the Trotters Independent Trading mindset. On a more personal

Not just a three-wheel van, but a clever marketing tool.
Oh yes, the punters saw us coming a mile off.

level, it denotes a character of high energy, enthusiasm and cheer; a dynamic, open and communicative person who breezes through life leaving a path of joy and positivity in his or her wake. I was also pissed at the time and it was very, very cheap.

After Raquel and me shacked up and it was time to become a two-car family, I went for something a bit more upmarket and bagged myself a Capri Ghia (sea-foam green, soft top, all the spec, only twelve previous owners, an absolute steal at four hundred nicker!). Since then I've had 'em all: a Rolls, courtesy of Rodney (the diamond in Mum's crown, I've always said it), Beemer, Jag, Toyota Yaris! Lovely jubbly!

In preparation for this book I got on the blower to my old pal Boycie, the 'go-to' man when it comes to all things vehicular in the Peckham, Camberwell and Lewisham districts:

ME: *Boycie, you made an absolute mint out of flogging jam jars. Tell me, how important is it in the world of business to have an half-decent motor?*

BOYCIE: *I didn't just 'flog jam jars' as you so eloquently put it. It was far more nuanced than that.*

ME: *Right. Now say that in English.*

BOYCIE: *My job was to source the right vehicle for the right client – something that would befit his or her status.*

ME: *Please explain.*

BOYCIE: *Well, take Trigger for example. What kind of vehicle springs to mind?*

ME: *A bath on roller-skates.*

BOYCIE: *You catch on fast, Derek. Then again, it doesn't always work that way. I still can't get over the time I sold a Rolls-Royce to Rodney. Rodney in a Rolls-Royce, dear God, it's like putting a tiara on Ian Beale. Fortunately the vast majority of my clientele were a lot more discerning.*

ME: *You mean they were snobs.*

BOYCIE: *Yeah. But I do seem to recall that I did a couple of transactions with you over the years.*

ME: *I'll never forget that Vauxhall Velox you sold me.*

BOYCIE: *Went like a dream, did it?*

ME: *Oh, it went all right, I just wish it would've stopped.*

BOYCIE: *Then you should have taken it up with my customer relations team. Anyway, the amount of times you stitched me up in the past, what did you expect?*

ME: *Brakes!*

BOYCIE: *What goes around comes around, Del Boy. I remember that*

A step upmarket. The Capri Ghia, circa 2001.

time I wanted to take an important client to watch Wimbledon and you said you'd get me the tickets.

ME: *And I got 'em, didn't I?*

BOYCIE: *Yeah, they drew nil-nil with Ipswich.*

ME: *That's your own fault for being so tight.*

BOYCIE: *Tight?! How dare you! I'll have you know that as a pukka Freemason I am involved in all kinds of local charity work, giving generously to the poor and the needy. I might not enjoy it, but I do it!*

ME: *Leave it out, Boycie, you're so tight you won't even tip your hat. I bumped into Marlene last week and she said you're still using both sides of the toilet paper.*

BOYCIE: *This conversation is over, Del Boy. Goodbye!*

ME: *Hold on, Boycie, I need to ask you something.*

BOYCIE: *What?!*

ME: *Will you write the foreword for my new book?*

BOYCIE: *(censored)!*

WARNING!

In this day and age of global warming, speed-bumps and metrosexuals, a lot of men are turning their backs on the motor vehicle in favour of bicycles. And while there's nothing at all wrong with this in principle, take it from me: no bird was ever knocked bandy watching a bloke unfold a Bickerton.

BUSINESS CARDS

Anyone who's anyone in the world of business carries that wonderful tool of self-marketing: the business card. A bit like having a stack of mini billboards in your pocket, the business card is an extension of you and your brand, and therefore a vital bit of kit for luring in prospective clients. That said, far too many are done poorly these days and most end up being filed with the geraniums. Make sure yours doesn't by following these two simple steps to creating a card worth keeping:

1. Include only key info on your card: company logo, name, job title(s), contact details, a catchy tagline and, if you're fortunate enough, a list of epidemic and/or personal achievements.

2. Go for a design that reflects you, your style and what you've got to offer. The trick is to elevate yourself above the competition by standing out from the crowd. I tend to opt for something that screams understatement, class and refinement, with just a subtle dash of danger.

If you're still in doubt, here're a few select examples from my own collection, just to give you a better idea:

Rodney Trotter

2 GCE's, DIC*, SOD**

*Diploma in Computerisation
**Senior Operations Developer

Email: **hot.rod@kwikmail.co.uk**

DIRTY BARRY'S
ADULT EROTICA EMPORIUM

Dirty by name, Dirty by nature

Call **0800 69 69 69**
and ask for Bazza.

TROTTERS ALL-STAR INTERNATIONAL TALENT AGENCY
(PECKHAM BRANCH)

Finding the stars of tomorrow, this afternoon!

Reputable agency representing only the crème de la menthe acts*

Auditions held every Thursday lunchtime at Burger King.
Call 07787 448 225 now and get a free Whopper!

Simon and Carbunkle, Spanner Ballet, A-Ha-Ha-Ha, Fine Young Cannonballs, Raquel Turner, and the singing dustman, Tony Angelino

---

DRISCOLL BROTHERS DIRECT

Business, property and kneecap insurance

'Here at Driscoll Brothers Direct we have a very simple philosophy: You pay us so we don't have to pay you.'
Guaranteed acceptance.
No medical questions.

Call **0800 60 50 80** and receive a free pen just for enquiring.

M. PEARCE PRODUCTIONS

Professional Photographer

Specialising in weddings, christenings, family reunions, Bar Mitzvahs and jelly-wrestling competitions.

Call **020 7242 4070** and ask for Mickey. If I'm not in leave a message with my mum.

PART FOUR
★★★★★★★★★★★★★★★★

TALK THE TALK

★

The way you talk is vital. Why say something is 'do-able' when you can say it's 'actionable'? Why say 'make the most of' when you can say 'optimise'? You might be thinking, *'Hold on, Del, now you're just talking bollocks.'* And you'd be right. But in this game it pays to talk bollocks. You see, modern business people don't talk proper English like what we do. They talk trendy 'business speak'. It's all about *platforms* and *initiatives* and *integrated structures*.

Confused? Don't worry, so was I at first. Here're a few pointers to get you started:

Action items = To-do list

Take it to the next level = Put your back into it!

Diversity = Curry or Chinese?

Open lines of communication = Chinwag

Maximisation = Make the most of (see optimum)

Touch base = What's occurring?

Wax lyrical = Rabbiting

Reach out = Oi!

Robust dialogue = 'Aving a barney

Black swan events = Cock-ups

Blue sky thinking = Using your noddle

Green field thinking = Using your noddle

An environment that encourages a free exchange of information = Pub

Time sensitive = Hurry up!

Executive burnout = Cream-crackered

Outsource = Get Rodney to do it

Exit strategy = Leg it!

Mega growth = Big/Uncle Albert's beard

Stratagem = Vitamins

Proactive = Margarine

Bottom line = Most importantly (my new favourite)

> ★ **OPTIMUM OPTIMISATION IS THE NAME OF THE GAME.**
> **IT NEVER HURTS TO TAKE IT TO THE NEXT LEVEL.** ★
> **BOTTOM LINE: MAXIMISE TO THE MAX!**

BUSINESS SPEAK

Now that you've got the gist of it, you can have fun and create some lingo of your own. For example, words ending in '-tion' are good business words:

Information

Integration

Penetration

Situation

Visualisation

➲ COLOURS ARE ALSO USEFUL:

Green

Black

Purple

Pink

Brown

Whatever takes your fancy.

➲ NEXT, ADD A THING, PLACE OR ANIMAL:

Wind

Cloud

Air

Gerbil

Bush

⊜ NOW MIX AND MATCH:

Black cloud information
Green wind integration
Brown air situation
Purple gerbil penetration
Pink bush visualisation

An absolute doddle! Try chucking some of these out the next time you're waxing lyrical round the water-cooler, and watch your colleagues' faces fill with envy that they didn't think of them first.

Top-quality merchandise. A rare security camera snap, courtesy of the Arndale Centre.

STATISTICALLY SPEAKING

Did you know that 84 per cent of business people who use statistics 72 per cent of the time in at least 60 per cent of their business dealings are 97.5 per cent more likely to achieve their goals? If you did, congratulations, you are part of a group of only 12 per cent of people who know that.

Statistically speaking, 100 per cent of what you just read was pure cobblers, but speaking statistically can give the impression that you've done your homework. Throw enough statistics out and 98.9 per cent of people won't have a scooby what's going on and will just accept what you're saying as fact.

INITIALS

Keep in mind that modern business loves initials. Think about it, you've got BP, M&S, HSBC, QPR, the YMCA. Unfortunately I came up with the name Trotters Independent Traders a long time before realising the importance of initials, and it weren't until I had some trendy headed notepaper printed up that the reality dawned on me. Still, I'm not embarrassed. TITCO (which is what I'll use from now on, just to save on the old ink and keep the editor sweet – blinding bird, she is, but you wouldn't want to get on the wrong side of her) is above all that.

MIND YOUR USPS

A USP (pronounced 'usp') is a Unique Selling Point, and it can be applied to either person, company or product. TITCO's USP – West

End goods at Southend prices, no questions asked – has remained simple and true to this day, but when it comes to specific products it's not always so clear-cut. Whether you're buying or selling, it's vital to identify the USP of the item in question.

Ask yourself:

- What problem does it solve?
- Does it save time?
- How will it change people's lives?
- Does it *save* people's lives?

When I came up with the idea for the 'Trotter Crash-Turban' I couldn't believe nobody else had thought of it. Day in, day out, Sikh motorcyclists were whizzing about completely unprotected, and nobody batted an eyelid. But eyelids were batting all over the place when Rodney and I presented the Crash-Turban on the *Dragons' Den*.

Now, I won't lie, the Crash-Turban (along with its sister project, the 'Burka-Buoy' – the first, and *only*, fully self-inflating burka) was a bit rough around the edges. That said, I still think the feedback from the Dragons was unnecessarily harsh. To paraquote Deborah Meaden, the idea was 'as concepts go, a complete and utter failure'. According to Duncan Valentine it was 'without doubt' the worst idea he'd ever seen. So much for constructive criticism.

The one and only real positive we took away with us came from Theo Paphitis, who said at the very least he admired our balls. For a moment I weren't too sure how to take this – what with the lights and the cameras I was already feeling a bit vulnerable. I don't want to go into too much ugly detail, suffice to say the whole thing ended

The Trotter Crash-Turban failed to set the world alight.

in a punch-up, which is why it was never aired on telly. It was hardly fair, though. There were five of them, plus security, against me and a Crash-Turban-wearing Rodney. We didn't stand a chance.

At the end of the day, and never one to dwell on the negatives, I have no regrets. And while you could say that the Crash-Turban itself crashed and burned spectacularly, I did manage to sell one to Trigger. He's not a Sikh and he ain't got a motorcycle, but, as he said, it's always best to keep your options open.

FRENCH 101

In the great melting pot that is the global marketplace, it's sometimes not enough just to speak English. You see, it's a well-known fact that 90 per cent of all foreigners come from abroad, so it goes a long way if you can speak at least one or two other lingos. It puts them at ease and, at the same time, lets them know they're not dealing with just any old Herbert. Luckily, as you've no doubt gathered by now, I've always been a dab hand when it comes to a spot of French (*al dente competente*). Maybe I got it from Mum. She was always a bit of a Francophobe. Whatever, don't panic, 'cos it's not as difficult as it seems. Here're a few quick phrases to help get you started:

Au revois = Hello/all right?

Bonjour = Goodbye

Mais-ouis = You're welcome/don't mention it

Mal de mer = First class/luxurious

Rez de chassis = All's well that ends well

À la bruschetta = Silly me/what a wally!

Très bien ensemble = Sense of occasion
('you've got no *très bien ensemble*')

Pas de basque = No, but seriously …

Nobless = Nobility

Bain marie = Exquisite!

Mon pleasuro = My pleasure

Potage bon femme = Need I say more?

Unison opportunaire = Meant to be

Mon dieu = Of course! ('*Mon dieu!* Why didn't I think of that?!')

Après moi le déluge = Everyone's a winner!

Bouillabaisse mon ami = No man is an island

Bonnet de douche = Top of the tree

Boeuf à la mode = Nothing ventured, nothing gained

Ménage à trois = Gordon Bennett!

Je ne sais pas pourquoi = He who sticks his nose into a beehive should expect more than a nostril full of honey

Bouchée à la reine = It is what it is

Conseil d'État = You scratch my back, I'll scratch yours

*Potage bon Femme? Me and Rodney doing our
bit for Anglo-French relations, circa 2002.*

Crème de la menthe = The best of the best

Fromage frais! = Eureka!

Duck à l'orange = Duck à l'orange (they copied us on this one)

J'adore un soixante neuf = I am enjoying this dinner

Drop a few of these into your next conversation, business or otherwise, and you won't fail to impress. Also particularly useful if you're dealing with a right sort. Trust me, it knocks 'em bandy!

★ **THE FRENCH HAVE A WORD FOR PEOPLE LIKE ME. I'M NOT SURE WHAT IT IS BUT THEY'VE DEFINITELY GOT ONE.** ★

SPIEL

As important as it is to be honest and upfront, a peppering of spiel never does any harm. After all, the customer expects a bit of window dressing. Whether you're flogging disposable lighters, Turkish raincoats or a vanload of weather-damaged butternut squash, at the very least you want the punters to walk away feeling like they've had an experience. But before that can happen you first have to get their attention. Now, there are many clever and intricate ways to achieve this but I've always found that being loud works best. And I don't mean go out and get yourself a megaphone – you don't want to attract any *unwanted* attention – just be loud enough to be heard within a fifty-yard radius. Aim for the ninety decibels mark, about the same level as the average lawnmower, and you'll be laughing.

When I take the floor down the market and let the old vocal cords off the leash, I sometimes like to think of myself as a lighthouse foghorn, and the customers – ships lost in the mist, if you will – are just crying out for guidance.

★ **DRAW THEM IN BY BLOWING THEM AWAY!** ★

PICTURE THE SCENE:

You're traipsing round the market hoping to find a bargain. You've browsed all the stalls offering the same old boring guff at the same old extortionate prices. There's a spit of rain in the air and you're feeling a bit cream-crackered. Time to call it a day. You turn to head off home when up ahead, through the haze of shoppers, you notice a well-turned-out, finely proportioned and dapper-looking geezer holding court. He looks both out of place and right at home all at the same time. You move closer. And then you hear it: *'Gather round, ladies and gents, 'cos at these prices I can't afford to deliver. Now, I've got a very special treat for you today, namely, these 36-piece canteens of cutlery! Hand-crafted in Indonesia using the finest steel and featuring these stunning ivory-effect handles, they also come with*

A face you can trust. Me in the market doing the bizzo, circa 1985.

this genuine synthetic-leather display case. Oh yes, in terms of quality we are talking the absolute titmus test! So much so in fact I have it on good authority that Her Majesty the Queen has this very same set in her Welsh dresser at Buck House. But, of course, she only gets 'em out for special occasions. The manufacturer recommends a retail price of £42.99, but thanks to free enterprise, bulk-buying and a mate of mine who does a bit of smuggling, I am able to let 'em go today – and today only, mind you – for £3.50!'

On fly-pitching duty circa 1989. A dynamic market force.

Naturally, you open your purse and snap one up. You're not a wally! The next day you see him again:

'Right, I haven't come here to be laughed at, chaffed at or generally mucked about, I have come here to sell my wares, and they're guaranteed to cure hard-core, soft-core and pimples on the tongue. Take a butchers at this: the Musta F80 in-car radio, as recommended by Nigel Mansell himself! Solid state-of-the-art technology direct from the leaders in the field of applied audio science, yes, I am of course talking about: Albania! It's got multiple pre-sets, synthesised tuners, digital scanning, auto-reverse equalisers, MW, LW, FM, LCD, ICI and B&Q, and it comes with two, count 'em, TWO, quadriplegic speakers! Yours for a tenner if you get in quick. Remember, I'm not here today – gone tomorrow, I'm here today – gone this afternoon!'

★ **BE A CUNNING LINGUIST!** ★

Some call it sales-talk, others call it patter, Rodney has been known to call it bullshit. I like to think of it as the tinsel on the Christmas tree, the currant on the bun, the shish in the kebab, if you get my drift. Whatever you call it, get it down to a fine T.

WARNING!

Don't lay it on *too* thick. It just so happens that subtlety is a forte of mine, and, coupled with a strikingly handsome but trustable face, it has rarely ever let me down. Having said that, there have been times where even I've come unstuck …

CASE STUDY #04

I'd managed to get my hands on a consignment of handheld deep-penetration massagers. Just to be clear here, I'm not talking about the kind of things Dirty Barry used to give away free with a set of handcuffs and a gimp mask. No, the Inframax deep-penetration massager was clinically proven – it even had the stamp of approval from the National Osteopathic Board of Surgeons (NOBS to you and me). Amazing really, considering it looked like little more than a brake light from an Austin Allegro that someone had stuck a handle on. But no, when it came to a vertebrae this bit of kit performed wonders!

And yet with all that, I couldn't flog 'em for love nor money. A new and more visual angle was needed – a demonstration. This

A technological breakthrough in back-pain management.
Not a brake light from an Austin Allegro.

is usually where Rodney would have stepped in but at the time he was busy helping out down at the local undertakers (leading the processions, causing ten-mile tailbacks, destroying their computer department, that sort of thing), and so with more than a smidgen of trepidation, I turned to Uncle Albert.

On the face of it, he was the perfect man for the job. You see, having spent half his life either holed up in crow's nests or squashed into life-rafts, Albert had always suffered badly with his spine. That was the good news. The bad news was that after one quick blast of the Inframax's healing rays the soppy old duffer started doing the hokey-bleedin'-cokey right there in the middle of the market! You can just picture it: one minute he was hobbling along like Old Father Time, the next he was giving Anton du Feck a run for his money! I'm just glad I stepped in before he did the moonwalk. I couldn't believe it, and more to the point, neither could the punters.

PART FIVE

★★★★★★★★★★★★★★★★

ORGANISATION AND CONTACTS

★

Did you know that human beings are capable of using only 10 per cent of their brains? Just think about it. At this pacific moment in time 90 per cent of your brain is sitting about scratching its arse like a spare one at a wedding. A bit frightening really. Of course, there are those rare and special few who are able to whack the percentage up a notch or two (Einstein, the late, great Steven Dorking, Vorderman etc), but they're the exceptions. It reminds me of the time back at school when a special team of quacks was brought in to assess Trigger's IQ. The final diagnosis, according to his Aunt Reen, was that Trigger was what psychiatrists call an 'idiot savant' (a bit like that Rain Man geezer in the film with Dustin Hoffman, I forget what it was called). The thing is, I saw those results and I couldn't see the word 'savant' anywhere. I didn't say nothing though; it was a very proud moment for Trig.

Where was I? Oh yeah. This being the case, it's no wonder that in the frantic one-hundred-decisions-per-minute world of modern-day business we can all too often feel a bit disorientalised. And that is why it is doubly important to have a carefully thought-out system in place.

FILING AND FAXING

If you can't afford a PA to organise all your appointments (and you ain't got an Uncle Albert hanging about), don't worry, you can always invest in a Filofax. I did back in the late eighties and let me tell you,

Notes

Africa

~~Petulia~~ 😊

~~does the business~~

1 x sweet and sour pork

1 x spare ribs

1 x special fried rice

Omelette for Albert

Appointments/
meetings:
Drop printing
round to Boycie.

Appointment: 9.30
a.m. – pick up wigs.

Reminders: Monday:
Call Gordon. Check
if he's still bald?

Reminders: Check –
what is a natural birth?

Potential baby names:

Troy
Arnie
Lance
Sigourney
Rex/Dex
Rodney

Shopping list:
tuna (x 8 tins)

Batteries
Castellas
Scotch

Always protect your investments.

it changed my life. Up till then I wrote most of my important notes down on beer mats or the backs of cigar packets. Since then this little book of mine, full to the brim with a list of all my contacts, hastily scribbled-down action items and minutes from meetings, has attained a sort of Holy Grail status around these parts – I've had to get it insured, it's *that* sought after. There's no telling what might happen if it got into the wrong hands.

And before you say it, I know that these days most people use their phones for this sort of thing, but I'm a traditionalist. Every dipstick and their uncle's got a phone. The Filofax is a bit special. It harks back to the golden era of the yuppie and singles you out as a serious player.

CONNECTIONS

It always helps to have friends in high places, and seeing as most of my mates live in tower blocks, I had a bit of a head start. *Pas de basque*, having the right contacts is a must for the upwardly mobile business entrepreneur. A quick flip through the contacts section of my Filofax will show you that I know the right person for every inconceivable eventuality:

Need a motor? **Boycie's my man.**

A driver? **Give Denzil a bell.**

Jewellery? **Abdul.**

Fashion? **Monkey Harris.**

Roofing materials? **Paddy the Greek and/or Sunglasses Ron.**

Emergency date? **June Snell.***

---

* This was, of course, back before I met my one and only true love, Raquel.

Printing? **Alan Parry.**

Electrical goods? **Ronny Nelson.**

Banking advice/loans? **Cassandra.**

Babysitter? **Mickey Pearce.**

Entertainment? **Tony Angelino.**

Entertainment of the adult variety/general smut? **Dirty Barry.**

Theatre tickets at short notice? **Limpy Lionel.**

Last-minute pump-action shotgun? **Higgy Higgins.**

Need to get rid of twenty-five barrels of toxic waste, no questions asked? **Where's Trigger?**

Heavy boxes need shifting? **Rodney.**

Someone to go and get the bacon sandwiches? **Rodney.**

Someone to wade waist-deep into a pond to capture a rare and endangered butterfly? **Rodney.**

I could go on, but you get the idea.

Knocking 'em bandy. Me leaning on my aluminium briefcase chatting to a couple of yuppie sorts, circa 1989.

NETWORKING

By the late 1980s, Peckham had become a very trendy area, and me, a regular face on the wine-bar scene. Oh yes, back then I could often be found holding court with the bistro-kids, discussing the merits of centralisation vs decentralisation with people with names like Adrian and Chloe. Having always loved the cut and thrust of a well-honed and honest argument, I was in my element. Of course, once a few of the old white-wine spritzers went down things could get pretty heated, and on more than one occasion punches ended up being thrown. But that's just par for the course. What mattered most was that I was getting out there and putting it about a bit, expanding my clientele, keeping my foot in the door and sizing up my competitors.

I remember a particular deal I put together that well highlights the importance of making the right connections. You see, I'd just heard on the grapevine that my mate Abdul's cousin's girlfriend's brother's mate's mate was a gamekeeper at a private zoo. '*Big deal,*' I hear you say. Well, hold on, I ain't finished yet. A couple of days later I heard that Monkey Harris's sister's husband's first wife's stepfather worked for an animal food company. Of course, it didn't take me more than a second to join the dots and come up with a pretty picture! Often the best deals aren't the result of careful planning. A lot of the time they just tumble into your lap like that. But that means being in the right place at the right time …

CASE STUDY #05

I'd treated the family to a nice day out in the country. There was an auction on and some boxes needed to be lifted, so it was lucky they were there. On this particular occasion I'd hit the jackpot with a gross load of figurine cats. Perfect examples of North Korea's prestige porcelain industry, they also revolved and played 'How Much Is that Doggie in the Window?' A triple treat for connoisseurs of fine china, music and moggies.

We were on our way back when we spotted a bird broken down at the side of the road. Never one to ignore a lady in peril, I told Rodney to pull over. A thorough examination of her engine confirmed my initial suspicion that her car was knackered, so I decided we should give her a tow. Like I said, I'm just old-fashioned when it comes to this sort of thing, and her revealing that she was in fact Lady Ridgemere of Ridgemere Hall (a big pile of country estate we'd passed a couple of miles back) had absolutely nothing to do with it.

Once we got her home safely her old man was falling over himself to show his gratitude, inviting us in for a cucumber bap and a sweet sherry, and while we were in a hurry to get off and beat the rush hour, it seemed rude to say no. Well, it weren't long before the old charm laser beams were knocking His Lord and Ladyshipness for six. Judging by the way they kept looking me up and down I got the impression they didn't get out that much – wafting about in that big old house by themselves, I must have been a much-needed shot of adrenalin to their systems. Bless 'em. Anyway, one thing led to another and we ended up getting onto the subject of art, as I so often do, and his Lordship was well impressed with my knowledge of all things Byzantine period. Meanwhile their butler, Wallace, a miserable old bark who looked like he'd been knocking about during the same period, plied the drinks.

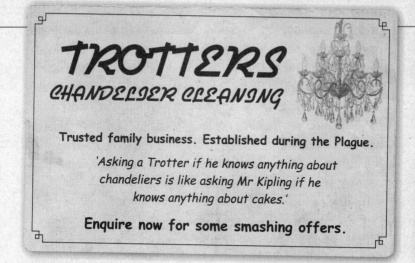

TROTTERS
CHANDELIER CLEANING

Trusted family business. Established during the Plague.

'Asking a Trotter if he knows anything about chandeliers is like asking Mr Kipling if he knows anything about cakes.'

Enquire now for some smashing offers.

With rush hour still pressing and not wishing to outstay our welcome, I gave it another hour and then insisted we get back on the road, but not before nipping out to the van to get one of the cats. I was on my way back when I happened to overhear His Lordship on the phone to some firm who'd promised to clean a pair of his chandeliers. I'd spotted the chandeliers on the way in and, well, these things were something else! Pukka seventeenth-century French crystal, they really were the Louis Louboutins of the chandelier world. Still, this firm was asking for twelve hundred sovs! By this point I'd taken quite a shine to the Ridgmeres, so I could hardly stand by and see 'em get ripped off. I'd never have forgiven myself. Besides, I knew we could give those chandeliers a decent buffing and still be smiling south of four hundred notes. The Ridgemeres knew it made sense, the deal was sealed right there and then, and as a gesture of goodwill I let 'em have the cat at cost.

'But you need specialist equipment for a job like this!' Rodney cried when we got back home. I quickly reassured him that I had no intention of doing a cowboy job. Knowing that once word of our value-for-money services got around we'd soon be a sought-after commodity amongst the dukes and earls, I was already seeing the bigger picture. A whole new world of opportunities was opening up in front of us.

'Come on, Rodders,' I said to him. 'It'll be like *Alex Through the Looking Glass!* You'll dine at the finest restaurants on steak chasseur and salute potatoes.' I could see him weakening so I pushed on.

'Your shoes will be made by Goochi, your jewellery will come from Asprey's, your clothes will be made by Man at C&A!'

He cracked.

'But we do a proper job, right? No bodging!'

I promised him the whole operation would be the very pinnacle of professionalism; as good, if not better, than that of the finest chandelier renovators in the land. I then nipped into the kitchen to see how we were doing for Windolene and Superglue.

The Ridgemeres were on holiday the day we arrived, but old Wallace was there to take care of us. He gave us the sort of welcome normally reserved for something rabid then shuffled off to dust the portico. Sensing that my skills were best served in a supervisory role, I got Rodney to set up and then sent Grandad upstairs to lift the floorboards and loosen the locking nut. Rodney and me then got into position on the ladders, a big canvas bag stretched out between us to catch the chandelier. Above us we could hear the bolt creaking as Grandad turned the spanner.

'One more turn, Del,' he called down to us.

In that moment I envisioned myself mingling amongst the dukes and duchessesses, glittering country set soirées, afternoons spent shot-gunning pigeons and galloping after foxes before heading back for a munch on a pheasant leg. Oh yes, it was the *mal de mer* lifestyle I was destined for.

Ridgemere Hall. What a choker!

The chandelier then fell … and kept on going.

You see, what Grandad had failed to mention to us was that while we were working on the first chandelier, he was working on the second one. Call it what you will – bad luck, a simple breakdown in communication or a cock-up of titanic proportions – the result remained the same: the chandelier, along with my vision, was shattered into a thousand little pieces.

Of course we did the right thing and hung about while Wallace got on the blower to the Ridgemeres. Feeling that the whole thing was partly my fault, I apologised profusely and thankfully they understood that these things can happen.

Oh, and I fully refunded them for the cat.

Where was I? Oh yeah, what I'm saying is that business rarely comes knocking at your front door. You need to cast a wide net to catch the juiciest deals. And just like the trawler men who use gut instinct to guide their boats to the right waters, you, too, should listen to your guts. And I mean that figuratively and literally. I ignored my guts once and it turned out to be an acute case of irritable bowel syndrome (see page 221).

Always keep an eye on your overseas markets. Me on the blower to Tokyo.

MULTI-TASKING

As the name suggests, multi-tasking is the ability to take on multiple tasks all at once – a vital skill-set in every conscientious yuppie's arsenal. It's a talent that my Raquel has in spades. Many's the time I've stood in wonder watching her whizz about cooking the dinner, tidying up *and* preparing a fresh batch of laundry for the ironing board, all at the same time. Like Orville, minus the Dean, it's a mesmerising sight. Not that I don't like to help out every now and then, it's just that she's so good at it I don't want to interrupt her flow and stress her out. My dear old Grandad was no slouch in the multi-tasking department, either. I can still see him now, sitting in his armchair watching *The Dukes of Hazzard*, eating a corned beef sandwich with one hand, having a good old dig about in a lughole with the other. Bless him.

WARNING!

Not all multi-tasking is good. Back in the late eighties, long before the advent of blue teeth technology, Rodney attempted to drive the van down Peckham High Road whilst simultaneously conducting a smoochy '*No you hang up first ... No, YOU hang up first*'* conversation with his girlfriend, Cassandra, on his mobile blower. The conversation was cut rudely short when he failed to notice a great big ginormous juggernaut pulling out of the

---

* He hung up first. He had no choice really as he weren't wearing a seatbelt at the time. The berk!

next junction and, due to a sudden but dippishly late attempt to correct his error, also the Ford Orion he ended up hanging out the back of.*

BOTTOM LINE:
★ ONLY A DIPSTICK DIALS AND DRIVES! ★

TOOLS OF THE TRADE

Whatever your area of expertise, you ain't gonna get very far if you ain't got the right tools for the job. In my game this means that I am rarely ever without my trusted blue suitcase. It's been with me through thick and thin and back again, and has still yet to let me down. Not only has it contained all of my various and wonderful wares, it makes for a decent seat, a handy display case, and it also once doubled as a mugger-stopping battering ram. A true multi-tool if ever there was one.

I can't tell you what tools (actual or meteorological) you'll need, that's for you to decide, but I would advise that you choose them carefully and don't blame them when things go Gok Wong. After all, a tool is only as good as the person using it. You should also strive to maintain your tools to make sure they stay in tip-top nick. A man

---

* Fortunately both the phone and the van were all right. Rodney came out of it with a red nose and a minor whiplash.

Colin Ball, a.k.a. Trigger. I've known a lot of blokes born an 'apenny short of a shilling but in Trig's case God added VAT.

who knows all too well the importance of this is my old mate Trigger. Not only is he extremely diligent in caring for and maintaining his tool of choice, he's actually won medals for it. Well, *a* medal. It's always better to get it from the horse's mouth, so here's a little interview I conducted with Trig on this very point:

ME: *So, Trig, tell me about your medal.*

TRIG: *It was the council's idea. They wanted to award local people for services to the community.*

Trig's proudest moment: winning a medal for outstanding achievement in broom preservation.

ME: *Cushty. What exactly was the award for?*

TRIG: *It was for saving the council money. See, one day I happened to mention to a local councillor that I'd been using the same broom for twenty years.*

ME: *Twenty years? That's a lot of sweeping for one broom.*

TRIG: *I know. But there's an old saying that's been handed down by generations of roadsweepers: 'Look after your broom.'*

ME: *And …?*

TRIG: *And that's it: 'Look after your broom.'*

ME: *I like that. It makes you think.*

TRIG: *Does it?*

ME: *No, not really. So tell me, how did you manage to keep the broom in such good condition in all that time?*

TRIG: *I changed the head seventeen times and the handle fourteen times.*

ME: *(silence)*

TRIG: *Receiving that medal was a very proud moment in my life. It's the sort of thing you tell your grandparents about.*

ME: *Yeah, well, it's always nice to get a pat on the back for years of hard work and dedication. I've got a Queen's Award for Industry plaque back at the flat.*

TRIG: *Ain't yours though, is it?*

ME: *No, course not, but I'm still proud.*

TRIG: *I like to think my medal was also a symbol of trust and recognition of good character.*

ME: *I'm sure it was. Well, I reckon I've got enough for now. Cheers Trig. You popping down the Nag's Head later?*

TRIG: *Probably not. I've gotta go round my sister's to arrange an alibi.*

ME: *Righto. Good luck.*

TRIG: *So I'm gonna be in your new book, am I?*

ME: *Course you are, I wouldn't leave a mate out, would I?*

TRIG: *I'll have to look at the book first.*

ME: *You what?*

TRIG: *I'll have to check it. It's nothing personal, I just want to make sure there's nothing I disapprove of.*

ME: *Don't be a plonker all your life, Trig. This ain't some Spot the Dog job. It's gonna be very wordy.*

TRIG: *How many words?*

ME: *I dunno ... about a thousand.*

TRIG: *A thousand words? Are you pulling my leg, Del?*

ME: *No, straight up. At least a thousand. It's a proper book, Trig. It's got an index, bullet points, soliloquims ... a spine, everything!*

TRIG: *That all sounds a bit too heavy for me.*

ME: *You know it makes sense.*

PART SIX
★★★★★★★★★★★★★

DOING THE DEAL

★

C hess, poker, draughts, Pokémon Go, whatever game you're playing you stand more chance of succeeding if you've prepared and have a plan of attack. The one I fell back on most over the years was loosely based on that of the Special Forces. Obviously I'm talking physiologically here; there was no abseiling involved or anything like that. Everyone's different of course, but I tended to do most of my deals the same way the SAS clear a building full of terrorists: with charm as my stun grenade, wit as my bulletproof vest and acumen as my ammunition, I used speed and surprise to get in and out before anyone knew what'd hit 'em. But that's just me. I'm the sort of bloke who would've captured German machine-gun nests.

SALES TECHNIQUE

I could sell rice to the Chinese, me. *And I have!* Back in the early eighties I managed to get my hands on a job-lot of water-damaged Uncle Ben's. I was also well in with the guv'nor of the local takeaway. Put the two together and what've you got? A nice little earner!

The key to sales is communication. You could be the brightest bod with the bestest ideas, but if you can't communicate, forget it! The key to communication is listening to your market. A lot of firms these days will fork out a small fortune on research and analysis, but I've never had to worry about it. I specialise in making dreams come true, that's my market, and *'what're you looking for?'* is the only question that needs to be asked. Nine times out of ten I've already got just the thing in the garage. If not, you can bet your life I know a bloke who knows a geezer who knows a mush who can get his hands on one.

Of course there are also times when people don't know what they're looking for and you have to help them along a bit, but that's all right, it just depends on how you approach it. Everyone's different, of course, but I prefer to do most of my deals on the go and in an informal fashion if I can. Stuffy office meetings are fine once in a blue moon, but the pubs and the clubs are where I hold most of my

Happy days. Me, Rodney and Albert unboxing another bargain of a lifetime.

conferences. And I don't like to take too much time when sizing up a deal. The decision comes fast. Not that I'm impatient (I ain't got time for impatient people), but 'cos I trust my gut. I know what'll sell, who my target market is, the right price *and* where to dump it if it goes belly up, all in the time it takes most people to fart.

When I do a deal I'm not just selling you my wares, I'm selling you a dream. But before that can happen I've not only gotta show you the dream, I've gotta make you *believe* in it.

Take a simple everyday object like a pen, for example. Nothing really that exciting about a pen, is there? Well, that depends on whose pen it is. You see, my pen ain't no ordinary pen: my pen is the groundbreaking technological miracle that is the *Dura-Last-Aqua-Nibbo-Pen-Ultra!* Not only is it unbreakable, it can write both underwater and in space! As if that weren't enough, it also glows in the dark, just in case you need it in a power cut! It is in fact the very same model Buzz Armstrong used up on the old lunar module. Well, he had to have something to write his postcards home with, didn't he? You see, I've got a mate who knows a bloke who's got a contact at NASA. I'm telling you, once you've tried the *Pen-Ultra*, your Bics and Parkers will become a distant memory. It usually retails at £9.99, but as I'm feeling in a good mood and I like the look of you, it's yours for a nicker! Can't say fairer than that, can I?

And there you have it. I'm down a Biro and up a quid, you've got the pen of your dreams and all is right with the world. *Par de Calais*, as they say in the Dordogne.

The fact is that what the punter wants more than anything else is a bargain. Take the Poundland business model as a perfect example. People scoffed at first. '*Everything for a pound?!*' they gasped. *'That'll never catch on!'* But it did. Now, if it had been me I'd have called it *Two-Poundland* and doubled my profits, but that's just splitting hairs. The point is that you can flog almost anything if the price is right. You just need to come at it from the right angle:

- *Briefcases that can only be opened by professional safe crackers?* More like Old English vinyl document holders for the security-conscious yuppie.

- *Manky-looking tomatoes?* Extra sun-ripened for a fuller flavour. And I'm letting 'em go at two for the price of three! What more d'you want?

- *Fur coat that looks suspiciously like tabby?* Nah, that's Epheopian mink, innit? You don't agree with the fur trade? That's all right, it's stimulated Epheopian mink!

Honesty matters, but you shouldn't let it get in the way of closing a deal. Rodney always tended to get bogged down with little details like facts and morals. Don't get me wrong, these are important, it's just that when it comes to buying and selling I'm a big believer in the never-say-never approach. Rodney approaches a deal the way most people approach a colonoscopy, humming and harring and thinking himself into a panic attack before finally deciding it's against his 'principles'. Then again, the times he did throw caution to the wind and stuck his neck out, the results were nothing short of diabolical: a shedload of broken lawnmower engines being one of his most memorable 'investments'.

NEGOTIATION

From a simple wage increase to a company buy-out, the art of negotiating is something every businessman and woman worth their salt needs to master. Some of us, like yours truly, have a natural flair for this sort of thing. It's a crying shame really that they didn't send me in to sort out the Brexit deal. I'd have had it done, dusted and rolled out all in time to get to the pub for a pint of Stella and a mussel sandwich. Yeah, those Euro gits wouldn't get so mouthy with me at the table. Not unless they wanted a smack in the mooey. Where was I? Oh yeah, some of us are born with this talent, but that don't mean you can't learn, hone and perfect the art.

For many, the thought of sitting down to lock horns at the negotiating table can cause a lot of anxiety (hives in Rodney's case), but it needn't be that way. Just remember these five basic rules:

Stay focused on the prize and go for the win-win

Understand what all parties need and work towards that. After all, the most satisfying deals are those in which everyone walks out a winner!

Be patient

A quick deal is always preferable, but the *right* deal is always worth waiting for, so be prepared for long talks. I negotiated a deal once that took the best part of *half an hour*!

Know your opponent

Knowing a little bit about the person you're negotiating with can go a long way. For instance, if you know they like a drink, catch them when they're in the boozer – all the better if they've had a right skinful as they probably won't remember any of it the next day.

If you're buying … Keep it short and sweet and don't be afraid to haggle.

Example:

ME: *How much?*

TRIG: *To you, Del Boy, seventeen quid.*

ME: *Five.*

TRIG: *Twelve.*

ME: *Six.*

TRIG: *Ten.*

ME: *Nine.*

TRIG: *Eight.*

ME: *Done!*

★   *FEARLESS + FIRM + FAIR = EVERYONE'S A WINNER!*   ★

Never appear too keen

Again, if you're buying, point out the flaws of the item up for grabs. If there aren't any, invent some – even better if you can get someone else to point them out for you.

CASE STUDY #06

Back in the late seventies, a mate of mine, Eddie Malcolm, got into the second-hand motor trade and opened up a site in a prime spot in the West End. I call him a mate but we had some history. I don't want to get into details, it was a long time ago, but suffice to say he stitched me up something chronic over a consignment of partially melted space-hoppers – two hundred quids' worth in total! Well, he went straight out of my good books after that.

Skip forward a year, I was on the look-out for a decent set of wheels and, lo and behold, Eddie had just the thing: a smashing little Mark 4 Cortina, one previous owner, four doors, sonic-blue paintwork, oh yes my son, it was the *crème de la menthe*! The trouble was Eddie was asking five hundred notes for it, which was a bit out of my price range. Never one to be perturbed by such minor obstacles, I gave the situation some thought and realised that I was being presented with a 42-carat, two-birds-one-stone opportunity. I'd been wanting to get even with Eddie over those hoppers and this was my chance.

In order to execute my plan, I needed someone's help, but it couldn't be just any old someone, it had to be a good friend; someone reliable; someone I could trust. Sod's law, they were all busy, so I got Boycie on board.

The next day I had a mosey down to Eddie's site. He chucked me the keys to the Cortina so I could give it the once over and then ducked back into the office to deal with another customer. At that moment Boycie pulled up in his brand-new Merc.

'Five hundred sounds reasonable to me, Del Boy,' he said, inspecting the Cortina.

'But look at it, Boycie,' I said, as the crook-lock from the steering wheel mysteriously came loose in my hands. 'Look at all the damage!'

'What damage?'

It was then, as I stepped back to let Boycie get a better look, and purely by accident, that the crook-lock whacked into the wing mirror.

'Well, *that* for a start!' I said.

Of course when Eddie returned I pointed it out to him.

'Who the bloody hell did that?' he said.

'Kids probably,' Boycie said.

Needless to say I wasted no time in telling him the whole deal was off.

'It's only a broken wing mirror, Del.'

'As far as we can tell, yeah,' I said, 'but who knows what damage they've done under the bonnet? I mean, be fair, Ed, you're asking top money for a motor that's been vandalised by a bunch of yobs!'

'It happened at my site once,' Boycie chipped in. 'The little gits put sand in the oil sumps. Completely knackered the engines.'

'Bloody hell,' Eddie said, turning it all over in his head.

'I wouldn't touch it if I were you, Del,' Boycie added.

'Yeah, you're probably right, Boycie,' I said. 'But Eddie's a good mate and I'm a gambling man, so I tell you what I'll do for you, Ed, I'll give you three-fifty and I'm putting my head in a noose.'

Eddie protested, then made a counter-offer of four.

'What, and then he's gotta shell out for a new engine?' Boycie said.

'I can't let it go for three-fifty,' Eddie insisted.

'You won't see it go at all if it's got sand in the sump,' Boycie reminded him.

Eddie mulled it over some more. I could see he was weakening and so I went in for the hard buy.

'Come on, Ed, make your mind up, I'm a busy man. D'you want a sale or not?' I pulled out the three hundred and fifty quid, a plump roll of crisp notes, and wafted it under his chin, 'Three hundred and fifty lovely spondulicks, in cash, we do the deal now.'

I knew I had him on the ropes, and sure enough a moment later he caved. He grabbed the dosh, we shook hands on the deal and he popped back into his office to get the log book. Meanwhile I jumped into my very own Ford Cortina.

'You owe me a scotch, Del,' Boycie said.

'I'll make it a double,' I reassured him as I inserted the key into the ignition and turned it.

Nothing happened.

I turned it again, and still nothing happened. At that point Eddie returned with the log book.

'Oi, Eddie, you got petrol in this?' I asked.

'Yeah, almost a gallon,' he said, looking just as perplexed as me.

'Pop the bonnet, Del,' Boycie said, 'one of your leads might have come off.' I popped the bonnet open and Boycie stuck his head in to have a butchers.

'It's not your leads,' he said as he began unscrewing the oil cap.

'Oh,' he said.

'What is it?'

'You've got sand in your oil sump, Del.'

There was no going back on it. We'd already touched hands on the deal. I'd just spent three hundred and fifty quid on a motor that needed a new sodding engine (which would set me back at least another two hundred!). So let that be another lesson for you. Before entering a deal make sure all your bases are covered, and above all …

ALWAYS CHECK YOUR OIL SUMP!

ANIMAL INSTINCT

Selling is all about the where and when. Think of it like one of those nature documentaries where a lion waits patiently in the undergrowth, keeping a careful watch over a flock of antelope. Well, the market is my undergrowth and the passing shoppers are my antelope. And just like the lion, I instinctively know the optimum moment to make my move.

Before I go on I should explain something. Many, many moons ago I had a little misunderstanding with a local magistrate, who then saw fit to take the law into his own hands and ban every council in London from issuing me a trader's licence. Being someone who trades in his sleep, this has always been an especially sharp thorn in my side. Still, I swore to myself from that day forward that I wouldn't let it hold me back, and it hasn't. All right, it has come with its own challenges, but there's nothing Derek Trotter likes more than a challenge.

★ *'ON DIRE TERRAIN, DO NOT LINGER.'* ★
SUN-TZU, THE ART OF WAR

For the last year or so, and on Damien's advice (he swears by it), I've been studying the book, *The Art of War*. Written two thousand years ago by some Chinese bloke called Sun-Tzu (sort of like the ancient Chinese version of Theo Paphitis), it's basically a tactical guide for battlefield success, but it can also be very useful when applied to the field of business. It does contain a few duds though, like '*Shouting at night is a sign of fear*', which is a bit of a given really. Still, in my case it usually meant Albert was having another nightmare about the Battle of the Baltic.

Going straight to the top, flat out!
Me, ready for another power lunch at the Berni Inn.

I think what Sun meant here was to choose your pitch carefully. If he'd asked my advice (and I'm sure if I'd been around at the time, he would have) here's what I would have told him: pick a spot at one of either ends of the market, preferably the one with the clearest escape route. If things go belly up you don't want to be stuck slap-bang in the middle of a busy market if you can help it. I find it helpful to be out of shot of any CCTV cameras (they make me come over all shy) and to have a carefully placed look-out to warn me of any approaching danger. Not because any illegal activity is taking place, heaven forbid, but you know what these people in authority are like, one little bee gets in their bonnet and they're out to ruin your day. I just prefer to do what I can to avoid giving myself that kind of headache, that's all.

It takes a bit of careful planning though. The old Arndale shopping centre, for instance. Always a favourite spot of mine, it was also more often than not swarming with security. But I couldn't help but notice that the guards regularly changed shift at midday and the new lot always started on the bottom floor, giving me just enough time to nip in and do a spot of business on the top floor. The guards were none the wiser, the punters walked away with a dream deal and I was up a bob or two. Everyone's a winner!

CUSTOMER CARE/DAMAGE CONTROL

We've all heard the old saying that the customer is always right and, I'm afraid to say, it's true. Whether you like it or not, when a disgruntled punter is doing his pieces right up in your boat race, sometimes you've just gotta grin and bear it, no matter how much you want to give 'em a clump. This is an area I've had a lot of experience in. As you've no doubt gathered by now, as skilful and accomplished a businessman as I undoubtedly am, I'm not King Minus and not everything I touch turns to gold. In short: I've had more comebacks than Cher!

The trick to dealing with a dissatisfied customer goes as follows:

- Remain calm.
- Be patient.
- Listen.
- And above all, spiel:

Dodgy-looking Albanian car radio that emits flames?
Well, you've taken it out of the box and mucked about with it. And I did chuck in a free Kylie Minogue LP. What're you moaning about?!

Perfume that smells like the aftermath of a fire at a cat sanctuary?
That's just the essential oils mixing with the musk. And it says 'Odour de Toilet' right there on the bottle. What did you expect?

An anatomically incorrect Action Man figure?
All right, so he's let himself go a bit, what d'you want for a nicker, jam on it? So what if he's got breasts? He's a non-binary Action Man!

An overcoat with a big hump in the back?
It's genuine *camel* hair! Sacred Blue! There's just no pleasing some people!

Then there are those times when no amount of spiel will smooth things over …

CASE STUDY #07

I'd done a deal for 125 top-of-the-range handheld hair dryers. Beautiful things they were: heavy-duty, solid handles, multiple power settings – the sort of kit Joan Frieda would have used. And so when I sold one to my mate, Mike, the landlord at the Nag's Head, and he ended up in A&E with a bonce full of blisters, I was absolutely mortified. Certain that he must have just pressed the wrong button or something, I got him a bunch of grapes and went to assess the situation.

That's when I discovered, to my utter dismay, that they weren't hair dryers, they were in fact electric paint strippers. After my initial shock had faded, I considered it further and quickly spotted the upside. All right, technically speaking they weren't hair dryers, but they did *dry* your hair, and safely (if you used the lowest setting and kept them at arm's length). And who don't want their hair to look nice while doing a spot of DIY?

Mike, who by this point had been told that his hair might never grow back, failed to see the silver lining. Feeling as though the whole thing was partly my fault, I made amends by giving him a full refund and a free wig. Couldn't say fairer than that, could I?

*Salt of the earth. Nag's Head landlord, Mike Fisher.
He made a blinding banana daiquiri.*

CAPTIVE AUDIENCE MARKETING

Captive audience marketing is the art of forcing your wares on people when they have little to zero chance of escape. If you've ever been to IKEA (where there's one entrance and one exit, about two miles apart from each other, meaning you've gotta trudge through the whole bleedin' store just to catch a glimpse of daylight), you'll know what I'm talking about.

But advertising, and all that is the power of suggestion, is big bunse. We live with it every day of our lives and have become so used to it we don't even notice it's there most of the time. Or at least we don't notice that we notice. It's a bit of a dark art really when you think about it (as I have done many times), sort of like the business equivalent of being subconsciously flashed – you weren't expecting to see it, you didn't wanna see it, but Gordon Bennett it was waved right in front of your face and there was nothing you could do about it! So it's no wonder that airport lobbies, medical receptions, football stadiums, cinemas, buses and trains – basically anywhere people are hanging about waiting for something to happen – are prime targets for this kind of brutal but effective hard-sale tactic.

While this has never been a core element of the TITCO business model, there have been a few occasions over the years when situations have presented themselves and I've taken full advantage …

CASE STUDY #08

I'd popped into the post office for a packet of stamps and a Pot Noodle. As I was standing there, trying to decide whether to go for chicken and mushroom or beef and tomato, I got chatting with a neighbour of mine, Mrs Obuku (lovely old girl, made a smashing goat curry). I can't remember what we chatted about (I'm talking early 1980s here), but it was all very pleasant.

I'd grabbed the chicken and mushroom and was making my way to the counter when, all of a sudden, a team of stocking-faced, shooter-wielding nutcases burst in and closed the shop. All told there was about five of us in there at the time, including an old mate of mine, Tommy Razzle. Of course we were all in a state of shock, but I told Mrs Obuku not to worry and got her a seat over by the greetings cards. I was thinking it would all be over in no time, but there must have been some problem with the safe, as almost a quarter of an hour later and we were still hanging about.

It was then that I noticed Tommy nervously picking at his watch strap, so much so that it broke. Well, I was doing a lovely line in Casio digitals at the time so I thought I'd have a punt and see what occurred. Tommy was reluctant at first, his focus fixed firmly on the geezer holding the sawn-off, but with a little pressing and a brief and whispered description of the Casio's unique design features, he saw sense and we shook hands on the deal there and then – well, we would have if we hadn't been ordered not to move.

CASE STUDY #09

Back in the early nineties we had an outbreak of riots on the estate. I remember it clearly as me and Raquel were going through a bit of a rough patch at the time. I'd been spending too many late nights at the casino, desperately trying to earn us a few quid, and she got it into her head that I was enjoying myself. I know. Crazy! Anyway, it got so bad that she ended up taking Damien and going to stay with Rodney and Cassandra at their flat.

I put on a brave face but deep down I could feel myself going under, and so I turned to two of my oldest mates for support: Johnnie Walker and Ron Bacardi. Thankfully Rodney talked some sense into Raquel and she gave me a bell. I was in the Nag's Head at the time and I can't tell you how joyous a moment it was when we sorted it all out over the mobile blower. I made a solemn promise to her there and then that the gambling and drinking was over and then ordered a bottle of champers to celebrate the reunion. Leaving the van at the pub I took a Toby home. I can't remember much of the journey but it was mostly diagonal, and I was so happy I burst into song.

When I finally got home I went straight to bed. A few hours later I awoke to sounds of carnage coming from down in the precinct: explosions, screaming, police sirens, horses neighing. It was a full-scale riot! God knows what caused it. Some gobby drunk more than likely. And yet with all this mayhem going on and my mind still fumbling beneath a fog of Bollinger bubbles, I still had the foresight to spot an opportunity.

You see, at the time I'd been trying to flog a consignment of ski gear: puffa jackets, gloves, bobble hats, goggles, the works. Made in Fiji – which, as anyone who knows their pistes will tell you, has always led the way in Alpine apparel (not just disposable cameras) – it was top of the range. I'd even got Rodney to model the gear down

Rodney modelling Fiji's finest down the market. He did look a bit of a tit.

the market, which, now I come to think about it, is probably why it weren't selling.

Anyway, at that moment, with the din of the baying mobs in my lugholes, I did what any sane and half-decent-minded entrepreneur would have done: I grabbed a load of the gear and went down to the precinct to conduct some business. It was a bit nippy that evening so I had little trouble getting shot of the jackets and gloves. Then the police started firing tear gas and I couldn't believe my luck. I must have outed at least fifty pairs of goggles in the first ten minutes!

Of course I had to keep on my toes. I'd been ducking and diving my whole life but nothing like this! Needless to say I ended up making a tidy little profit. Looking back now I s'pose I was a bit like the Kate Adie of the business world. But that's just the sort of bloke I am. When there's a deal to be done it takes more than tear gas and a few Molotov cocktails to stop Derek Trotter.

The original Trotters Independent Traders dream team, circa 1981.

*Rodney. Not much cop when it came to financial advice,
but the boy knew his way around a pencil.*

Sorting out passport photos, circa 1984.

The Jamaican Swallowtail (papilus humorous). Poor sod.

Topping up on some oily brain-grub. Me Rodney and Albert in Margate, circa 1989.

Into the nineties with a smart new image.

Damien. We went through hell squeezing him out, but it was well worth the stitches.

Here're some I flogged earlier...

Wigs of distinction...

Peckham Spring mineral water...

Musical china cats...

...and robust Russian camcorders.

You gnome it makes sense.

The single-greatest deal we ever made. Due to my foresight and business knowledge, I knew this Victorian egg timer (which I stumbled upon during a house clearance back in 1981) would come up trumps 16 years later.

SOTHEBY'S
Founded 1774

Sotheby's Auction House's London,
New Bond Street, Sussex,
London, Olympia

Ref: TR/56384/02

RECEIPT OF SALE

Harrison, John

Session - 1 47578
Date of Auction : 23/6
Auctioneer - T Cuthbertson
Lot Number (73 of 162)

Mr Derek Trotter & Mr Rodney Trotter
Flat 127 Nelson Mandela House
Peckham
London

Auction of Lot 73

John Harrison - H6 Solid Silver Pocket Marine Time Keeper

Lot No.	Reserve	Starting Bid	Reserve not met	Final Bid	Final Bid
	150,000.00			6.2 Million	

Sotheby's Auctioneers & Valuers
Founded 1744

Raquel and me enjoying the fruits of my business brilliance.

Giving back to the community. Me, Liz, Rodders and Phil.

Everyone at the Nag's Head came out in support of our plight.
Left to right, Sid, Trig, Boycie, Denzil, Marlene and Mickey Pearce.

Cassandra, Rodders, me and Raquel, circa 2003.

PART SEVEN
★★★★★★★★★★★★★★★★★★★★

TECHNOLOGY

★

I t's vital in business that you keep your ear to the ground and your foot in the door. Trust me, in the financial jungle things change thick and fast. What was in yesterday is out today and what's in today will be out tomorrow. It can give you the right hump. Take the world of toys for example. Back in the 1960s we all marvelled at Meccano. In the seventies the Etch-a-Sketch took the art of doodling to a whole new level. In the eighties there was a collective gasp at the Cabbage Patch Kid. In the nineties our minds were blown wide open by the Mutant Ninja Turtle. Nowadays sprogs are spoilt for choice: X-pods, Wii-boxes, i-Stations and all sorts of mind-boggling electronic thingamabobs. When I was a nipper a conker and a bit of string was enough to keep you busy for hours. A yo-yo was a thing of dreams!

Bottom line: you've gotta be willing to go where the wind blows you if you want to stay ahead of the competition. And while it's true that in my time it blew me all over the place, one pacific area in which TITCO never failed to make its mark is technology.

VORK SPRUNG DIRK TECHNIC

If you'd have told me back when I was first starting out in this game that one day in the not-too-distant future we'd all be watching flatscreen tellies and talking to each other via statallites, I would have probably laughed and called you a dipstick. If you'd have told me that one day

I'd end up having a barney with an Echo Dot, I would have told you to seek professional help. But that's what happened when Rodney got me one last Christmas. In case you're still a bit wet behind the ears, an Echo Dot is one of those plug-in devices you ask questions and some electronic sort named 'Alexa' answers 'em for you.

Things started off well enough: a bit of light flirting, a few French phrases, she was well impressed. Half an hour later and she started getting shirty, claiming she couldn't understand my lingo and asking me to repeat myself umpteen bleedin' times. By the end of the evening the moody mare was giving me the cold shoulder. I thought it best we sleep on it but she still had the face-ache the next morning. I ended up pulling the plug and giving her to Trigger, and he's never been happier – I saw him in Argos last Friday looking at the engagement rings, so it must be serious.

All that said, TITCO has been at the forefront of some of the biggest and most groundbreaking technological innovations of the last half-century: pocket calculators, microwave ovens, home solariums, the Furby … You name it, we've flogged it!* Our first major inroad into the wonderful world of integrated disc drives came when I did a deal with Ronnie Nelson for fifty personal home computers. These things weren't any of your old Japanese rubbish either – oh no – The R.A.J.A.H.-500 was made in Mauritius (not much cop when it comes to dodos but magicians with a megabyte!). Pukka-looking machines they were too. I mean they had all the little buttons and flashing lights and what 'ave yer.

---

* I was even one of the first to buy shares in Sinclair C5.

Naturally, I thought we'd make a killing. The problem, as I discovered when I got 'em home and was testing out the latest Pac-Man, was that they had this habit of switching themselves on and off whenever they felt like it. I hold my hands up, this wasn't ideal, but for the price I was letting 'em go for I felt it could be overlooked. The other problem, which Rodney discovered a couple of days later when he was in the middle of doing his homework on one, was that they had a tendency to heat up quite quickly. Now, this don't sound too bad on the face of it; after all, it's not unusual for electrical appliances to warm up a bit when they're used, but when they start to leave grill marks on your tablecloth, you've got a real snag on your hands.

Luckily I had my very own I.T. department in Rodney so I got him to investigate the issue. He flicked through the instruction manual, gave the R.A.J.A.H. a whack, and returned his verdict: 'These things are up the wall!' A more scientific explanation would have been nice, but he had a point. It weren't my fault, though. I gave the manual the once over before I bought 'em but it was all in foreign! How was I to know? Still, despite everything, I did manage to offload one to the local firm of undertakers.* Cushty!

Rodney embraced the technological change wholeheartedly and it weren't long before he set about attempting to computerise the whole business, something that made me feel more than a bit uneasy (all those years I'd spent trying to limit a trail of sensitive business-related 'data' and there he was shoving it all onto a microchip!). He even joined an evening class just to brush up on his RAMS and ROMS and ended up studying for a 'diploma in computerisation'. It meant a lot of homework and it did interfere with business, but he was learning and I supported him all the way (I gave him a lift to class if and when I could and always made sure he didn't forget his dinner money). After a few stumbles he finally bagged the diploma. As an added bonus he also met his future wife, Cassandra, in the process. What a boy!

Oh yes, TITCO entered the technological age with a bang. Literally in some cases.

---

* It went out of business two short months later, but that was purely coincidental.

THE INTERNET

If you want to survive in the volatile world that is twenty-first-century business, getting the hang of the internet is an absolute must. Now I admit, as dynamic and adaptive a bloke as I am, it took me a while to get my head around this. Then again, most of my business acquaintances don't really have that much of an 'online presence' (except for Dirty Barry, but we won't go there). Trigger, for example, still struggles to walk and whistle at the same time, so you can just imagine what he must make of a Yahoo!

Thankfully I had Damien to teach me the basics. Having grown up with things like modems and Wikipedicures, nothing fazes that boy. He's also very well versed in what is known as 'cyber-speak'.

From: Derek Trotter
To: Damien Trotter
Sent: 24/9/2011 at 12:01

Oi Damien. You should have been down the Nag's Head last night. You missed a minor miracle!

From: Damien Trotter
To: Derek Trotter
Sent: 24/9/2011 at 12:02

What happened?
Did Trigger get Rodney's name right?

From: Derek Trotter
To: Damien Trotter
Sent: 24/9/2011 at 12:02

No. Boycie bought a round!

From: Damien Trotter
To: Derek Trotter
Sent: 24/9/2011 at 12:02

OMG I literally cant even right now.

From: Derek Trotter
To: Damien Trotter
Sent: 24/9/2011 at 12:03

What? Stop talking like a moby.

From: Damien Trotter
To: Derek Trotter
Sent: 24/9/2011 at 12:04

Sorry Dad.

And of course I also have Rodney, which, with all those years he spent fiddling with his floppy disk, is like having my very own Bill Gates on speed-dial. Then again, even Rodney can come unstuck. Many's the time I've heard him moaning that his inbox is full of Spam. I dunno, he always was a messy eater. Bless him.

WARNING!

As much as I'm a fan of it, the internet is a whole other universe of weird lingo, slang, short-form and anacronyms that can leave even the most computer savvy scratching their filberts.

From: Derek Trotter
To: Rodney Trotter
Sent: 3/2/2010 at 11:14

Rodney what does WTF mean?

From: Rodney Trotter
To: Derek Trotter
Sent: 3/2/2010 at 11:15

What the f***

From: Derek Trotter
To: Rodney Trotter
Sent: 3/2/2010 at 11:15

All right I was only asking. Moody git!

Rodney always loved playing with his joystick.

And that brings me neatly on to another wonderful feature of the digital cornucopia that is the modern age ...

EMAIL

Every once in a blue moon a discovery comes along that blows the bloody doors off the van of convention and changes the world for ever. For anyone old enough to remember handwriting, the arrival of the email was one of those discoveries. On a par, I'm sure, with the arrival of sliced bread or the first ever packet of Monster Munch, it took the headache of finding a pen and a piece of paper – physically writing words down – bunging it all in an envelope – licking the envelope – licking the stamp to whack on the envelope – and then popping out to find a letter box, and kicked it all into the long grass with the simple touch of a button.

WARNING!

You have to be very careful and responsible when using email, especially in a work setting. One simple slip of the finger can cause serious ructions ...

CASE STUDY #10

Back in the late noughties Rodney took to working from his flat. He'd developed a serious bout of what psychiatrists call 'angoraphobia'. I assumed this meant he'd suddenly become terrified of cardigans, but it turns out it actually means a fear of the outdoors. Being the sensitive and understanding bloke that I am, I did everything I could to ease him out of his shell, but no amount of telling him to get his arse into gear and calling him a tart would help. He simply refused to step foot outside his front door, and to this day the whole episode has remained a complete mystery.

Fortunately, Rodney's phobia made its appearance just one week after I'd made Damien an official and key member of the TITCO team. The boy was brimming with energy and ideas and eager to let loose (a real chip off the old block) and so Rodney's absence didn't cause too many problems.

Anyway, it was during this period that Damien, for a laugh, emailed Rodney a little internet clip that was, well, let's just say: somewhat inexplicit. I really can't go into detail about its contents (this book might end up on a shelf in Asda!). Suffice to say it was in Russian and involved a ping-pong ball and a bucket. I came over a bit tom-dick when I saw it as I'd just that second finished eating a bacon sandwich.

Still, we all had a good giggle and thought that would be the end of it. Rodney then went to delete the email but instead pressed a 'forward-to-all' button. Well, you can just imagine how Cassandra and her mum and dad felt when they opened the message up, saw the words *'Here, have a butchers at this'* and pressed the play button. To make matters worse, Cassandra, who had recently rejoined her old bank and was working her way back up the ladder, was just about to give a very important presentation when she pressed it. God knows what she did to him when she got home but when Rodney arrived at

*Cassandra. When it comes to banking, badminton
and moules mariniere, she's in a league of her own.*

ours later that night with his suitcase in hand he was as white as a
sheet (and for someone who's always been only one shade short of
albino, that's saying something).

Of course he blamed Damien, a big fight erupted and I had to
step in to mediate. Damien, in his defence, said he was just trying to
cheer his uncle up, but as Raquel rightly said, the whole debacle was
disgusting and degrading to women. Damien got a verbal smack in
the ear and was docked a week's wages and two short months later
Cassandra calmed down and Rodney went home.

On the upside, Rodney's phobia disappeared overnight. *Rez de
chassis*, as they've been known to say in Grenoble.

But it's not always like that. A lot of the time I like to use email just to 'touch base':

From: Derek Trotter
To: Rodney Trotter
Sent: 18/4/2000 at 14:02

All right Rodders. What you up to?

From: Rodney Trotter
To: Derek Trotter
Sent: 18/4/2000 at 14:03

You know what I'm up to.
I'm sitting three feet away from you.

From: Derek Trotter
To: Rodney Trotter
Sent: 18/4/2000 at 14:04

Blinding bit of kit this email lark, ain't it?

From: Rodney Trotter
To: Derek Trotter
Sent: 18/4/2000 at 14:04

Cosmic.

From: Derek Trotter
To: Rodney Trotter
Sent: 18/4/2000 at 14:06

I reckon I'll do most of my communicating this way from now on.

From: Rodney Trotter
To: Derek Trotter
Sent: 18/4/2000 at 14:06

I'm trying to get some work done here.
Stop messaging me!

From: Derek Trotter
To: Rodney Trotter
Sent: 18/4/2000 at 14:07

I'm only saying hello. I won't bother in future.

From: Derek Trotter
To: Rodney Trotter
Sent: 18/4/2000 at 14:12

Was that your stomach grumbling?

From: Rodney Trotter
To: Derek Trotter
Sent: 18/4/2000 at 14:12

Yes!

From: Derek Trotter
To: Rodney Trotter
Sent: 18/4/2000 at 14:13

Do you fancy a bacon sandwich?

From: Rodney Trotter
To: Derek Trotter
Sent: 18/4/2000 at 14:14

I am feeling a bit peckish.

From: Derek Trotter
To: Rodney Trotter
Sent: 18/4/2000 at 14:14

Good boy. Do me one while you're at it.
Cheers.

From: Derek Trotter
To: Rodney Trotter
Sent: 18/4/2000 at 14:15

Rodney?

Me with my personalised PC.

SOCIAL MEDIA

A great way to socialise without actually having to leave your house or look at or talk to anyone, big business loves a bit of social media. As far as I can tell, the point of it is to let the world know what you're doing and when and how you're doing it at any given moment. Oh, and don't forget to include photos of yourself as you're doing it. '*But what if my day-to-day existence ain't all that impressive, Del?*' I hear you say. Don't worry, 'cos the beauty of social media is that even if the thing you're doing is boring and completely pointless, you'll be guaranteed a couple of 'OMGs' and at least one 'I love you babe!' Happy days!

Apparently it's also vital to keep everyone up to speed by dishing out other bits of interesting personal info. Nothing *too* personal, mind you, just your age, birthday, where you live, what you drive, where you shop, what you wear, who your mates are, who you're dating, who you vote for, when and where you go on holiday, what you like and dislike, a general overview of your family history and a brief rundown of what you're having for dinner. So just the basics really.*

Finally, don't forget to make your opinions matter by getting them across on 'platforms' like Twitter, undoubtedly the quickest and most effective way to date to make very brief but insightful comments on important world issues, like celebrity weddings, celebrity deaths, celebrity plastic surgery mishaps, celebrity sexual misconduct cases, the state of Donald Trump's syrup and global warming.

---

* Sounds a bit dodgy, I know, but don't worry. After all, if you can't trust a giant faceless personal information-gathering machine, who can you trust?

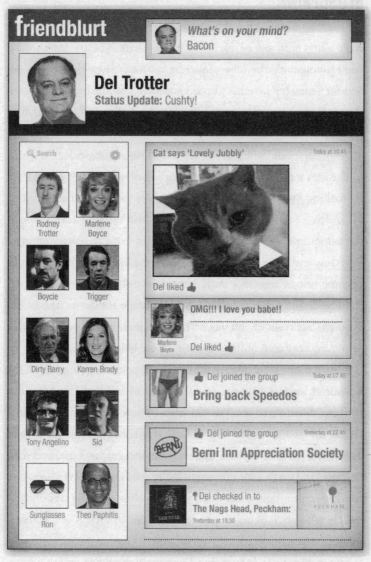

My social media page – a hotbed of first-class social activity.

BLOGGERING

All the rage amongst the 'online community', bloggering is when you write about stuff you're interested in and share it on the internet. I'd been toying with the idea of getting a bit of bloggering under my belt for years, but it weren't until I started off on the business lecture circuit that an angle presented itself to me. I weren't too sure at first and didn't really know what to expect, but I was on the internet anyway and, well, 'when in Rome' as they say in Düsseldorf.

The idea was to take my new role as business guru to the next level by making myself more accessible to those in the most direst need of guidance (and to make a shedload of dosh through advertising at the same time). Now, I'm no philosophist, but I've always enjoyed thinking, and since I started giving lectures I like to think I've already become one of the UK's most important public thinkers – not up there with the greats like Jeremy Kyle, Judge Rinder or the Loose Women, but certainly on par with Gary Lineker. And so, last year, I set up my very own online business advice blog: 'Dear Del'.

Well, it didn't take long for the queries to come flooding in and, for a while at least, it went very well. So well in fact that I had to close the blog down three short weeks later. I know what you're thinking: *'What are you going on about, Del? What you just said is a total oxomoron!'* Let me explain. You see, demand got too high, and with that demand came a lot of responsibility. Not that I've ever been one to shun responsibility, but when you're dealing with the emotions of people who are looking to you for solutions to their woes, there's a lot of pressure involved.

In the end it got so bad that I was seeking advice on my advice. That's when I realised I had to step away. Offering guidance is one thing, but when you leave yourself open 24/7 it becomes a right pain in the arse! All in all the whole experience gave me newfound respect for Claire Rayner.

Dear Del
Last month I fell off a ladder at work and broke my hip. I've been advised to seek compensation but I'm not sure how to go about it. What would you recommend?
W. Smith of Tooting

A new ladder. As luck would have it I've got just the thing in my garage. Packed to the rafters with the latest in grip technology, it's the safest ladder on the market. It retails at £45.99. You can have it for a score.

Dear Del
Are you the same Derek 'Del Boy' Trotter that back in 1989 sold me a mobile phone, the automatic aerial of which blinded me in one eye?
P. Williams of Guildford

No. That was a completely different Derek 'Del Boy' Trotter.

The welcome page to my Dear Del Blog.

URGENT ATTENTION: The Manage Direct of TIT
STRICTLY CONFIDENTIAL!

Greetings my friend,

My name is Prince Obasi Abubakar and I am boss man of large
Nigerian oil corporation (Nigerian Oil Corp PLC). It is real pukka
company that is plan to drill 250 new wells here in area well
known for oil. We are looking for UK firm to be partner in this
new and exiting venture.

Each well can make 1,000 barrels of oil and so this will be
very big 200% profit for you TITS. To be partner you must wire
us 3,000,000 of your English quids so we can get land rights for
drill. Once we are received with money we will email drill plan
and make lots of lovely jubbly.

Please reply urgent. No waste for time. For speed please also
send telephone number and address of residence and number
of passport and date of birth and full bank account detail.

You know this make sense my son. Yes?

Yours in prosperous
Prince O. Abubakar

*First off, I like the cut of your jib. I won't lie, as deals go this one
sounds right up my street. The problem is I'm a bit short on funds
at the moment. I could put together a little consortium of close
and trusted associates, but even then we'd be talking 2k max.
Tell you what, put two barrels aside for me and let me kip on it.*

Dear Del
Big fan of your blog.
M. Hartley of Romford

Thanks. Do you need any advice?

Dear Del
No.
M. Hartley of Romford

Dear Del
I'm the assistant manager of the Lewisham branch of Homebase.
Last week you came to the branch offering to give a lecture to my
staff, after which your yellow three-wheel van was seen backing
into my silver Peugeot 508, causing damage to the cost of exactly
£125.55. Please advise me on how you intend to pay for this?
P. Bailey of Wimbledon

*I don't know what you've been smoking mate but I'd give it a
rest if I were you. That could have been anyone's yellow three-
wheel van. Nice try though.*

Dear TIT

2k is good but need more for big drill. You not understand urgent of plan. Must act now with sending detail of your bank. In Nigeria we have saying: man who wait too long is serious idiot.

Yours in prosperous
Prince O. Abubakar

Sorry pal, prince or no prince, keep talking like that and the only thing you'll get from me is a doughboy in the eye. Do you think I was born yesterday? I ain't giving you a penny until I've seen the goods.

I'm starting to think you're not taking this seriously, Abubu my old China. Don't you see the wonderful opportunity staring us in the face here? Listen, I can get you the money but I'm a busy man and it ain't gonna be cheap. I'll need at least a grand upfront to cover my travel expenses, air tickets, a decent curry, that sort of thing. Send me the bunse plus a photo of the barrels and then we'll start talking. Can't say fairer than that, can I?

Dear Del

No it was definitely your yellow three-wheel van. It had the name 'Trotter' written in big black lettering on the side of it.

P. Bailey of Wimbledon

Automatic reply: I will be out of the office for the next six months. If your enquiry is urgent please email my customer support team at Boyce.ha@gomail.co.uk

---

Dear Del

My wages regularly turn up late and short. Every time I bring it up I always get fobbed off with a quick excuse. It's driving me up the wall! Please help!

I know this is you, Rodney. Go and stick your head in the food blender.

Dear Prince Abukabubu

Are you gonna give me an update on these barrels or what????

PART EIGHT
★★★★★★★★★★★★★★★★★★★

ATTITUDE
★

As you've no doubt gathered by now, I've had my fingers in a lot of pies over the years – a diverse goulash of ventures, you might say. But if I had to narrow it down I'd say that TITCO's core business interests have been, and are, in entertainment and lifestyle, telecommunications, healthcare, fashion, food and beverages, electronics, home improvement, travel, toys, stocks and shares, imports, exports, antiques and assorted knick-knackery. Which, when you consider that at any one time there's been no more than three of us manning the pump, is quite an achievement in itself.

But none of this would have been possible without first having the right attitude. It's often been said that Trotters Independent Traders put the 'tit' into attitude (see what I did there?). And for good reason. You see, I've always been a keen student of the art of PMA. Not to be confused with PMT (Pre-Minstrel Tension), PMA stands for Positive Mental Attitude, and having one is a must if you're gonna get anywhere in this game.

'*But how do I get a positive mental attitude, Del?*' I hear you ask. Well, I'm just about to tell you. If you stopped interrupting I'd get to it a lot quicker, wouldn't I? First of all, send off for my latest motivational DVD, *Get Positive, You Dozy Twonk!* (£10, cash only, no refunds, PO Box 14058, Peckham). Filmed in HD 4K Ultra, it's basically two hours of me driving around Peckham talking to all the people whose lives were deeply impacted by my PMA over the years. '*Sounds a bit conceited, Del,*' you might say, to which I'd say,

'*Too right, and thank you for noticing. Conceited is my middle name, innit?*' The point is it'll give you an in-depth run-down of everything you need to know about attaining and maintaining the right mindset to succeed. For now though I'll just break it down into a few easily digestible chunks for you.

KEEP AN OPEN MIND

It's very easy to get tunnel vision in this business, which is why I've always made a point of being flexible to new possibilities. My portfolio speaks for itself. If I'm not pitched up in the market banging out quality goods at knockdown prices, you'll find me in the pubs and auction houses, ever ready to grab an opportunity when it arises.

Fire-damaged woks? *I'll have a butchers.* A one-seat see-saw? *Why not?!* Musical doorbells that play thirty-six different national anthems? *Put two hundred aside for me.* Act as middleman between two moody Indians arguing the toss over some grubby old religious statuette? *A doddle!*

DON'T BE AFRAID TO STEP OUT OF YOUR COMFORT ZONE.

★   *REMEMBER: HE WHO DARES WINS.*   ★
HE WHO HESITATES ... DON'T!

One of TITCO's first outings into the service industry came about when my mate, Denzil, got hitched. His bride-to-be, Corinne, was a demanding sort who set very high standards, so when it came to organising the catering for the big day, Denzil turned to me. I'll be honest, I was hesitant at first, but Denzil being a mate in need, I caved (I dunno, he always had a way of wrapping me right round his little finger). I offered him a quote he couldn't refuse then me and Rodney set about putting together a buffet, the likes of which would've given Charles and Di's a run for its money. And all right, we ballsed it up in the end and everyone had to make do with pie and chips and a slice of jam sponge, but it still went down a treat and you wouldn't spot anything was amiss in the wedding album snaps.

Actually, that's not completely true. If you looked very closely you could see that Corinne's grin was just a partially disguised grimace. At the time I was too busy swinging a couple of bridesmaids round the dance floor to notice. But then I nipped to the bogs and Corinne saw her chance to corner me. Well, I couldn't possibly repeat here what she said to me, but it was quite hurtful and she gave it to me in full stereo. What worried me most, though, was that at the time she was still holding the knife that cut the sponge. I remember turning my head to look for Rodney, but all I saw were his legs disappearing out the nearest window. He must've gone to hide in the back of the van with Denzil.

Just when I thought it was curtains, and by the grace of God, the vicar emerged from the khazi and I seized my chance to escape. A lot of people would have been put off by this, but not me. It takes more than a fridge full of manky nibbles and a psychotic bird in a wedding dress to stop Derek Trotter.

We branched out again when Boycie and his missus, Marlene, mentioned they were looking for someone to look after their new puppy, Duke, while they went on holiday. Duke was more than just a puppy though. You see, Boycie and Marlene were struggling to get pregnant at the time. This would have been about 1984, so things like artificial dissemination, test tubes, ovums and all that lark were still very much in the early development stage. I won't go into too much detail, it's all very personal and none of my business, but it turned out Boycie was lacking somewhat in the tadpole department. To be more precise, he had what tadpole experts call 'lazy swimmers'. What made it doubly tricky in Boycie's case was that not only were they lazy swimmers, they were also doing backstroke. Apparently his doctor reckoned it had something to do with tight pants. Anyway, like I said, it's all very personal and none of my business, so I'll leave it at that.

Where was I? Oh yeah. This being the case, Marlene was feeling especially broody and so she looked upon Duke as being her little 'baby'. He required personal, round-the-clock care and attention, which, as luck would have it, I was more than able to provide at sixty quid a week. (I went in at eighty-five but Boycie wouldn't hear of it.)

Our first shock came when we went to pick Duke up and discovered he was a Great Dane. There we were thinking it was gonna be a chiwowwow or one of them little poodle jobs. Gordon Bennett, this thing was like a slightly undernourished horse! Of course, Marlene was almost in tears when it came to say goodbye. I reassured her that her 'little Dookey-Wookey' would receive nothing but the best care and attention, then we slung him in the back of the van and said *bonjour*. We got home all right and, apart from a slight panic in the lift when Duke mistook Rodney for a lamp post, everything was going smoothly. (Actually, Duke took quite a shine to Rodders – both being a bit gangly and soppy, I think they had a kindred-spirit

Boycie. More front than Brighton and tighter than two coats of paint.

thing going on. He weren't too keen on Albert though; he probably saw the beard as a territorial threat.)

Anyway, a couple of days later Duke slipped into a coma. I can't take any personal responsibility for this one. You see, after the vet's original diagnosis of Sam-and-Ella poisoning, we discovered that Rodney had simply mixed up Duke's vitamin pills with Albert's sleeping pills. The plonker! But no harm was done and, after a brief stint in rehab, Duke was back to his old self. On top of that, Boycie and Marlene were none the wiser and we still got paid (we even had a bit left over after sorting out the vet bills). As an added dollop of icing on the cake, Albert's beard had never looked so full and shiny. *Petit dejeuner!*

TREND SPOTTING

As I said, one thing you can be guaranteed of in the world of commerce is change. Markets change as times and people's needs and tastes change, and if you want an edge over your competitors you've gotta be ever-vigilant to these fluctuations. Successful entrepreneurs don't just follow trends, they predict them before they've even emerged. You might be thinking, '*Bloody hell, Del, how am I s'posed to do that?*' Don't worry, there're no crystal balls involved, all you've gotta do is get out into the world and pay attention. Talk to your customers and devour information in all its forms; go to shops and restaurants, watch films and read books. I make a point of reading two books per year (sometimes two and half and once *three*!), but like I said, I'm very cultured. If you're paying close enough attention, though, you'll notice the little telltale patterns.

Of course there are times when a trend will come completely out of the blue and take everyone by surprise. Coffee for instance. Who in their right mind would have thought takeaway coffee would catch on? But it did, and now you can't turn a corner without seeing a Starbucks or a Costa Coffee or a Café Wossname – it's wall-to-wall frappuccinos out there! But if you find you can't predict an emerging trend, and you can't be arsed to come up with your own, don't panic, you can just jump on one that already exists.

CASE STUDY #11

A classic episode in the life of Jesus Christ was when he turned water into wine. You can just imagine the shock on the onlookers' faces and, I've no doubt, the symphony of 'Gordon Bennetts' that rang out. Without wishing to get too sacramental, I've often thought that Jesus and I are similar in many ways. I don't mean looks-wise (I've never had a beard or nothing) but we both wanted to make a difference, we were both often misunderstood, and we both had books written about us. I didn't turn water into wine, though. I turned it into dosh!

Allow me to explain: I was pottering about one day on Grandad's old allotment, rotating the spuds, irrigating the mulch, all that game, when I heard a trickling noise. At first I thought Uncle Albert was having a Nelson Riddle behind the shed, but, upon further investigation, I noticed the trickle was coming from out of the ground. In short: I'd only gone and discovered one of nature's most rarest and precious wonders: a *spring*!* There have been a good few times over the years that I've felt gobsmacked, but never was my gob so smacked as it was at that moment. A natural spring in Peckham, right slap-bang in the middle of Grandad's grubby old allotment! Well, you couldn't make it up.

PECKHAM
Spring Water

1 litre ℮

BOTTLED AT
SOURCE

STILL
From an Ancient Natural Source

PECKHAM
Spring Water

SERVE CHILLED

The purest Peckham spring water, drawn from an ancient natural source discovered by returning Crusaders 800 years ago.

The spring is ideally located where prevailing winds and a protected environment together ensure a purity unique among spring waters.

Peckham still is a crystal clear spring water, delicious on its own or mixed. The diet conscious will find this pure low sodium spring water irresistible.

TYPICAL COMPOSITION

---

* The natural watery sort. Not a metal one.

All hands on deck. The Peckham Spring production line in full swing.

Standing there staring at the spring, I came over a bit spiritual. I was thinking of just leaving it be and keeping it a secret all to myself. I dunno, it just didn't seem right to interfere with something so ancient and pure.

Then I had another idea: why not exploit it to the max by putting it into bottles and flogging it? By pure coincidence, this was exactly round about the time that people were turning away from their taps and digging deep into their pockets for water of the bottled variety, so the market was wide open.

In terms of scale and reach, Peckham Spring mineral water has been my biggest venture to date. I got a certificate of purity from the SWANS (Spa Water and Natural Springs) committee, a loan from Cassandra's bank, pukka bottles, the full monty! In business parlance you could say that I was taking it to the next level, or, to be more precise: I was implementing systemically integrated brand-driven platforms all over the shop!

It weren't long before we were shipping Peckham Spring out to some of the most prestigious restaurants and hotels in the land. The punters lapped it up, the readies rolled in and it looked like it was gonna be a two-legged turkey for the Trotters that Christmas. I was on the verge of seeing my dream of one day becoming a millionaire finally become a reality. Little did I know that a great big sodding black swan event was lurking right round the next corner.

It all started when the water board began investigating what they suspected was a major underground leak on the estate. This, for

Solly Atwell. A brilliant legal mind, specialising in pleas of temporary insanity.

reasons never conclusively proven, in or out of court, led them straight to Nelson Mandela House and right up to my front door. That was when the nasty and wholly unfounded rumours began to circulate. It was all very ugly and slanderous, but the gist of the rumour was this: the spring on the allotment was just a hose pipe that I'd covered with mud and rocks and the true source of Peckham Spring was the tap in my kitchen. I know. Un-bleedin'-believable! It was like Eels on Wheels all over again, just on a much bigger scale and with water instead of fish!

I tried to push on but ended up in court staring at a charge sheet longer than Trigger's broom. By that point no amount of damage control was gonna cut the mustard. My lawyer, the late, great Solly Atwell, reassured me that since the spring on the allotment had mysteriously dried up just as quickly as it had sprung up, the evidence against me was flimsy, but he advised me to enter a plea of temporary insanity just in case.

Bottom line: I was in a right pickle. I turned to Rodney for support but him and Cassandra were already halfway to Cambodia. So, as I often do in times of trouble, I went to see Mum and told her all about it. She'd never let me down in coming up with a well-honed and common-sense solution in the past and, sure enough, as I sat there in the cemetery, a breeze picked up and, in it, I could hear her voice whisper: 'Bribe the judge, Del Boy, bribe the judge.' As luck would have it I didn't need to, and one week later the case was thrown out due to lack of evidence.

A lesser entrepreneur would've been put off by all this, but it takes more than a summons and a damning report from the World Health Organisation to keep Derek Trotter down. If anything it just made me even more determined.

DON'T HESITATE ... INNOVATE!

Whichever way you look at it, the world is full of serious problems that refuse to go away: unemployment and poverty; war and famine; Go Compare adverts and Tony Blair. It's a total nause! Thankfully when it comes to business, the majority of problems can be solved using that most important of all the tools at your disposal: that thing between your ears. No, not your hooter, I'm talking about your brain.

The fickle nature of supply and demand means that the marketplace is constantly shifting, stirring and churning, a bit like Rodney after a vindaloo. That being the case, a healthy company is one that rolls with the punches and adapts and innovates. The trick to innovation is understanding your customers' individual needs. Or, in business speak: '*Enabling an integrated stratagem driven by a global industry ecosystem resulting in a core culture of organisational reach and revenue maximisation.*'

Despite his two GCEs and his love of 'cross-cancelling equations'(see below), Rodney usually took a surprisingly simplistic and often negative approach to finding solutions to business-based conundrums. And while there's nothing at all wrong with having a swift and blunt exit strategy in place, not every problem can be solved by chucking it in a river.

Problem: We are traders who have nothing to sell.
We are traders who have no money to buy with.

Answer: We need to find a way to make money out of nothing.

Rodney actually needed ink to come up with this.

CASE STUDY #12

Back in the eighties (Grandad was still with us so it must have been early eighties), I'd got myself lumbered with 150 technicolour woollen tea-cosies. God knows what I was thinking. I must have got a whack on the head at a car boot sale or something. What with the invention of the electric kettle and the microwave oven, there just weren't much call for the cosy any more. I could've dumped them. I could've given them away free with a lovely line of near-perfect cut-glass goblets I'd recently picked up down the auction. But I didn't. I held on to them, trusting that a solution would present itself.

And that's when I happened to bump into a neighbour of ours, Mrs Murphy, out on the landing. She was a lovely old girl, Mrs Murphy, and only a month earlier she'd agreed to act as a test subject for a new range of orthodontic slippers I'd got my hands on. Anyway, I can't remember what we chatted about (something to do with her feet playing up, I think), but she happened to mention that she loved a bit of knitting. And that's when the answer came to me in a blinding flash. I got Mrs Murphy to stitch up the spout holes on the cosies then whipped them down the youth centre and flogged them to the West Indian lads as soppy hats. Mrs Murphy got a nice few quid for her troubles (and I let her keep the slippers free of charge), the lads down at the centre were happy as Larry with their stylish new headpieces, and I had enough left over to treat Grandad to a box of strawberries and myself to a Ruby Murray. *Petit filous*, as they say in the Dominican Republic.

CASE STUDY #13

One of TITCO's first decorating jobs came when we were hired to do up the kitchen of a local Chinese takeaway, The Golden Lotus. Nice place, did a blinding prawn ball, but the kitchen looked, and smelled, like an explosion in a dripping factory. The owner, Mr Chin, was doing his pieces. You see, he'd recently received a phone call from a health inspector warning him that if he didn't sort it out sharpish he'd be put out of business. I know what you're thinking: since when did health inspectors give tip-offs to their targets? It had us baffled too. I dunno, it must have been a health inspector with a heart, either that or it was some sort of divine intervention. The inspector didn't leave his name or anything so it will forever remain a mystery unfortunately.

Anyway, when I heard this bit of news I couldn't believe it, as it just so happened that I had a job-lot of paint in the garage that I was desperate to get shot of. What were the odds, eh? (Yeah, definitely divine intervention.)

Mr Chin shut up shop for a few days and I sent my interior design department in to work its magic. The only hiccup we had was a little bit of a disagreement about the colour the walls should be. Old Chin was adamant they should be blue. 'I like blue!' he said, making it very clear that blue was the way to go in his book. Problem was the paint was gold. When I explained to Chin the thinking behind this – that I chose gold merely to complement the name of his fine establishment – he knew it made sense.

And that was that. I let Rodney and his apprentice (Grandad) get on with the job. Slopping up grease and slapping paint on walls have never been my strong suits. Rodney's the artist of the family and I didn't want to get in the way of his vision, so I busied myself elsewhere. A couple of days, and golden coats, later, and the job was done. Chin coughed up the dough and everything was right in the world. Rodders had even managed to do an half-decent job by all accounts.

We were back at the flat, I was divvying up the wages, when Trigger showed up bearing some deeply disturbing news. It turned out the paint we'd used had been 'alf-inched a month earlier from a British Rail storage shed.* And this *was* news to me! If I'd had the slightest scooby I never would have touched it! Trigger then went on to explain that this particular paint was what they used for signs in tunnels. As if this weren't bad enough, Grandad then posed a very important question. 'How can you see a sign in a tunnel?' he said. 'It's pitch black!' And he had a point. The answer to this puzzling little enigma was that this weren't no ordinary paint. No, this was industrial-strength, *luminous* bleedin' paint!

By this point my old April was doing a locomotion of its own, but before the panic could really set in, the phone rang. It was Chin, and he weren't in a good way. 'What have you done to my walls?!' he cried. I had a bit of trouble hearing what he said next, he was quite emotional, but apparently the gist of the message was that his kitchen was *glowing* somewhat (and it was – you could see it from our balcony if you stood on tiptoes).

Thinking on my feet, quick as a flash, I set about laying down a spot of ad-lib damage control, explaining to him that what he was now looking at was a new range in energy-saving paint, designed pacifically to cut down on the old electric bills. It was desperate. It was a long shot. *It worked!* He even wanted us to go round the following week to do up his front room. Sadly it didn't happen. As much as it's nice to save on energy and cut your outgoings, it's also nice to have a dimmer switch. Chin lasted two nights in his new kitchen before a bout of temporary blindness set in and he decided blue was best after all.

* A true case of black cloud information if ever there was one.

THINK BIG

Like the changing of the seasons and the tides of the sea, life is full of mysterious and age-old questions. If a tree falls in a forest but nobody's around to hear it, does it make a sound? Are we alone in the universe? What colour is Paul McCartney's hair?* And of course – does size matter?

In broad terms, and as I've repeatedly told Rodney over the years, size doesn't matter, it's the thought that counts. In the world of business, however, it's a different story. Be it a jet plane, an elephant or a saveloy, let's face it, everybody prefers jumbo. And that's why, as a general rule, I always think big. It's a simple philosophy really: if you're gonna think of things, you might as well make 'em big things, or, as they say in the Mont Blanc district: *du pain, du vin, du Boursin.*

★ *FABRIQUE BELGIQUE!* ★

Back in the late eighties I was riding the crest of the yuppie tsunami. It was full-on, the mobile blower never stopped ringing, but I was doing the business and knocking knees bandy left, right and centre. Things were also on the up for Rodney. Him and Cassandra had got married and moved into a new flat, he'd got his diploma, and on top of that he'd been offered the position of heading up the computer section at his father-in-law Alan's printing firm.

---

* Aubergine would be my guess.

Rodney and Cassandra's big day, 1989. I won't lie, I did shed a tear or two.

Needless to say, this put Rodney in a very difficult spot. It was tearing me apart to see the conflict in him as he struggled to reach a decision, and so I made it for him. Obviously it wasn't easy to let him go, but after an extensive and exhausting search, I finally found a suitable replacement to fit the Rodney-sized hole. And while Albert did moan a bit at first, he did his best.

Anyway, for their first-year wedding anniversary, Rodney and Cassandra held a dinner party at their place. Cassandra was herself in line for promotion at the bank she worked in, and so she invited her boss, Stephen, and his wife. Rodney didn't take to Stephen, which, given that Cassandra was smooching up to the bloke looking to gain

Brownie points, was understandable really. All evening long Rodney sat there sneering at him. I was pleasantly surprised, though. All right, he was a bit of a prat, but it was clear from the get-go that when it came to business, Stephen knew his onions. He was a yuppie of the highest order (even though he very modestly denied it when I pointed it out to him), he played baseball during his 'downtime', holidayed in the Serengeti and had his finger firmly on the pulse of the global market. We got on like a house on fire.

It was towards the end of the meal, we were necking brandies, trying to wash the taste of Cassandra's moules mariniere out of our gobs, and talking shop. It was then that Stephen made a very important point, so important in fact that I later made a note of it in my Filofax. He was banging on about the stock market and future, long-term investments, and apparently 'Africa' was the key to the big bucks. I played it cool but made a quick mental note. According to Stephen 'growth' was the name of the game and Africa was all set to do some 'left-field proportion' growing in the not-too-distant future.

'Take the banana crop alone,' he said, 'we are into mega growth!'

Makes perfect sense, I thought. I mean, the bigger the banana the better. And I told him this. He looked a bit confused so I clarified my position.

'Well,' I said, 'it's easier to sell bigger bananas than little' uns, innit?'

He let it sink in and, I've no doubt, made a note of it in *his* Filofax when he got home. Overall I was well impressed and I think it's safe to say the admiration and respect was mutual. It's just a shame Rodney ended up punching him on the nose.

What Stephen understood, as did I, was that in this game you've gotta think big. And I don't just mean big ideas. I mean: *big!*

CASE STUDY #14

I'd done a deal with my old mate Ronnie Nelson on a consignment of Russian-made hand-held camcorders. This was round about the time that Jeremy Beadle had captured the nation's hearts and imaginations with the television show *You've Been Framed* (a title that always struck a nerve as it reminded me of the time the Old Bill planted six gas cookers in my bedroom).

The first thing I noticed about these particular camcorders was the sheer size of 'em. Big, sturdy, heavy-duty machines they were – always a sign of quality. I'm not sure of the exact specifications, the manual was all in Russian, but I'd say each one weighed about the same as a small adult woman or a tall and obese sprog. Rodney, who's always been left wanting in the shoulder department, was the first to complain. Of course I was quick to explain the unique selling point (USP to those in the know, see page 73) that with this bit of kit not only could you film your mates falling down flights of stairs and walking into doors (and receive one hundred sovs from Beadle himself for the bother), you could also give your upper body a good workout in the process.

It was a couple of days later that Ronnie explained to me that the camcorders were in fact designed for military use only. *Well, that explains the camouflage design*, I thought to myself. Concerned as I was (we don't get that many tank battles in Peckham), I was still, on the whole, unperturbed and certain that we'd make a killing. Rodney then discovered that the tapes the camcorders used were too big to fit in the VCR, and that did put a slight downer on the whole deal. I hunted about Curry's and Dixon's looking for a cheap Russian VCR, but drew a blank. I ended up flogging a few but had nothing but comebacks. The only one who didn't complain was Trigger, although I later found out that he didn't own a VCR anyway. At the end of the day it was a classic case of *bouchée à la reine*, as they say in Paris Saint-Jemima.

NEVER STOP BELIEVING

★ *'YOU'VE GOT TO HAVE A DREAM.*
'COS IF YOU DON'T HAVE A DREAM,
HOW'RE YOU GONNA HAVE A DREAM COME TRUE?' ★
MUM, ON HER DEATHBED

I'll never forget those words. Partly 'cos Mum was right, and partly 'cos years later I heard the *exact* same words in the lyrics of a song. I forget what song now, but it just goes to show how wise and insightful my mum could be. Must be where I get it from.

When Columbo set sail to discover the new world, do you reckon he turned back when things got a bit choppy? And what about our very own Nelson, eh? When he lost an eye do you reckon he said, '*Sod this, shipmate, I'm going home to bed*'? No, he whacked on a patch and went straight out to give the Armada a clump! To survive in the world of business, you, too, have to find some of that bulldog spirit, 'cos the law of averages dictates that things won't always work out as planned, and sometimes even your bestest ideas end up going for a burton.

Long before the *Changing Rooms* craze struck and people couldn't get enough of watching Carol wossername and that floppy-haired tart going around nauseing up strangers' front rooms, TITCO had its own designs on the field of top-class interiors at affordable prices. Well, what with Grandad's stint in the decorating game and Rodney's GCE in art, it was only natural we'd have a dabble. Not that we didn't take it seriously though. We had big plans at one point. We even set up an offshoot company, Simply Trotter Designs.

It didn't take off, but then not all hatchlings are destined to soar. What matters most is that you keep bunging 'em out of the nest.

> ★ **REMEMBER:**
>
> *WHEN LIFE KNOCKS YOU OFF YOUR HORSE,*
> *GET STRAIGHT BACK ON AND START PEDALLING!* ★

CASE STUDY #15

When Grandad passed away (he died), Rodney and me were cut to pieces. Then Grandad's estranged brother (our great-uncle) Albert turned up, and we were distraught! Albert was an old naval war hero who'd seen more underwater action than Flipper, and he was looking to stay a couple of nights just while he sorted out some digs at a seamen's mission. The arrangement must have fallen through 'cos sixteen years later and he was still at the flat. Well, before long he just sort of took over where Grandad had left off, working for the firm on a kind of part-time, substitute-teacher basis.

Dear old Uncle Albert. He never missed an opportunity to tell us all about his days at sea. It was like listening to the adventures of a coy carp.

This was round about the time that Rodney, in all his infinite wisdom, went full dippy mode and decided to blow the company's entire capital on a consignment of suntan lotion. *'Don't sound too bad, Del,'* I hear you thinking. Yeah, but at the time Peckham was experiencing the kind of freezing temperatures not seen since the dinosaur said *bonjour* to this mortal curl! And there I'd been hoping that a bit of my acumen would have rubbed off on him.

Anyway, I was down the Nag's Head drowning my sorrows when who should walk in but Brendan O'Shaughnessy (he was Irish). Brendan was a painter and decorator and was his usual jovial self. But this time he had a good reason. Over a Guinness he told me all about a contract he'd got to decorate and fit out a new housing estate over at Nunhead. My old spidey senses were already off the charts by this point, but I played it cool, got him another pint and continued to dig. And that's when I struck gold! You see, Brendan mentioned that the architect of this new estate was after fitting the whole place with louvre doors: 166 in total. At the time my mate, Teddy Cummings, managed a joinery works that specialised in, among other things … louvre doors!

I whacked the drinks on the slate, jumped in the van and wheel-spun out of the car park faster than a bluebottle with its arse on fire. I was well in with the Cummingses so I was expecting good news and, sure enough, Teddy offered me as many louvre doors as I wanted at the kind of mate's rates that would see us make 200 per cent profit on each. It was like Santa had arrived early – with a sleigh-load of louvre doors!

The snag (and in my experience there always is one) was that Teddy would only sell the doors in bulk and needed to seal the deal by the following Friday. We had a week to raise two grand! Well, we tried everything. We even asked for a loan from the listening bank, but they went mutton. Then Rodney had a brainwave. He warned me that it was a long shot, but in my excitement I was overcome by this sudden hope that the time had finally arrived for his GCEs to kick in and save the day. He then pulled out a magazine and told me all about a poxy rare butterfly that some divvy collector was willing to fork out three grand for. Despite this (and Albert's suggestion that we rent Rodney out as a sort of bargain-basement gigolo) all was not lost, as that very same day we bumped into Denzil down the market. He'd recently been made redundant and, being the wise and trusting bloke that he is, he agreed to loan me his redundancy money – all £2,000 of it.

We shot straight over to Teddy's, handed over the dosh and, along with his brother, Tommy, began loading up the stock. Later that afternoon, with the doors secured, we were celebrating back at the flat when I gave Brendan a bell to let him know the good news. And it was then that we came up against another, even *bigger* snag. Brendan informed me that the architect had now changed his mind and no longer wanted louvre doors. Just to make matters worse, we then discovered that Denzil's brothers were hunting us down looking to get his £2,000 back.

It was at this point I started to feel a nosebleed coming on. There was nothing left to do. We slung Albert in the back of the van and went to hide out at the cemetery.

As I said, I always like to be closer to Mum in times of trouble, and at least we could get a bit of peace and quiet there. Now, you're probably thinking, *'Why are you telling me all this, Del?'* I'll tell you why: because even after *all* these setbacks, with a garage jam-packed with 166 louvre doors that no git wanted and a gang of irate Rastafarians after our blood, I *still* hadn't stopped believing!

And that's when a minor miracle happened ...

The Lamborghini of headstones. Mum's monument, circa 1985.

It was that butterfly from Rodney's magazine, flitting about the headstones without a care in the world. It was our big chance to put everything right. Seizing control of the situation, I assigned Rodney the role of chief butterfly hunter, and after a few close calls and a dip in a pond, he finally managed to cup the butterfly in his hands. Back on dry land, Rodney, Albert and I stood there marvelling at this most beautiful and precious of God's little creatures as it made itself at home on Rodney's palm. After all that we'd been through, it was a moment I can only describe as ... well, metaphorical.

Just then Denzil came rolling along on his skates and, naturally, I didn't hesitate to tell him the good news.

'Denzil,' I cried out. 'We've got your money!'

'Great,' he said, slapping his hands down on Rodney's in a sort of upside-down high five. 'See you down the pub later.' And off he rolled.

We were flogging louvre sodding doors for the next fourteen months!

Petit Suisse.

FORTUNE FAVOURS THE BRAVE

One of the biggest and most common of obstacles you'll ever face, in business and in life, is fear. Whether it be a little nagging voice of doubt in the back of your head or a full-blown April-pouting panic attack, it can be very persuasive in stopping us from reaching our full potential.

Ask anyone who knows me and they'll probably tell you that I don't know the meaning of the word 'fear'. *'Del? Afraid? Pull the other one!'* they'd say. *'Rumour has it that Del once fell into a vipers' pit. He came out wearing snakeskin boots.'* But that's only 'cos I cover it well. The truth is that I feel fear just as much as anyone. Always have.

> ★ **'WE HAVE NOTHING TO FEAR BUT THE FEAR OF NEVER HAVING TO FEAR FEAR ITSELF.'** ★
> SOMEONE FAMOUS

The thing to remember is that it's natural to feel doubt and fear sometimes. It's not nice, I know, but trust me, it's nothing compared to the sting of regret and missed opportunity. The trick, if you can pull it off, is to harness the fear and make it work in your favour.

One of my most favouritest mottos is 'he who dares wins'. But I don't just say it. I *live* it! And while to a casual onlooker it may appear as though I'm just crashing in without a single thought for consequences, it's not only an approach that has served me well over the decades, it's one that was born out of necessity. Back when God smiled on Mum and made her die, and then Reg buggered off for the hills, I had a very important decision to make: put Rodney into care and bugger off to join Reg on the hills, or stand my ground and keep what was left of the family together. Of course, I chose door number two. Not only had I made a promise to Mum to look after her little Rodney, I also made a promise to myself that no matter how hard things got, Derek Trotter would be the man that Reg Trotter could never be.

REMEMBER:
STAND YOUR GROUND. RUNNING AWAY
ONLY WEARS OUT YOUR SHOES!

In business, just as in life, there will be times when you, too, reach a fork in the road and you're faced with two options: a) the road well travelled, or b) the one that ain't. You could always take the easy path and join the back of the queue. Or you could take the difficult path and end up broken down on the side of a roundabout in the arse-end of the sticks where no sod lives. But then you could do what I prefer to do in the above situation, which is to whip out a machete and a stick of dynamite and blaze a brand-new trail straight through the middle (creating a three-pronged fork in the process). It might be risky but as long as you keep your mince pies peeled for thorn bushes and poison darts, at the very least you'll end up with your own road.

Bottom line: don't be a sheep on a conveyor belt. Be a pit bull in a JCB!

> ★ **'WHEN A FORCE HAS FALLEN INTO DANGER, IT CAN SNATCH VICTORY FROM DEFEAT.'** ★
> SUN-TZU, *THE ART OF WAR*

Old Sun was spot on again with this one. In this crazy old world we call business, there are often times when you feel like you're under an endless bombardment of black swan events, each one blacker than the last – the gits just keep on flapping at you. Sometimes you might well feel like saying *bon douche* to the whole affair. *Don't.* The good news is that even an entire legion of the blackest and flappiest of swans can be successfully defended against with a well-disciplined and wisely placed battalion of blue ocean thinking. That's business speak for: hold your horses, 'cos you never know what's coming around the next corner.

CASE STUDY #16

Back in the mid seventies us Trotters suddenly found ourselves on particularly stony ground. I'd been well off my game (bird troubles most probably) and had entered a losing streak, and no matter how hard I'd tried, I couldn't find a way out (see Ikea, page 126). It got so bad that I was struggling just to put the egg and chips on the table. I turned to the one thing in the flat that I knew could earn us a good few quid and save our bacon. It was an antique globe that Mum had left us. It meant the world to us, it really did.

So you can imagine how painful it was when, out of desperation, I organised a raffle with the globe as the star prize. It broke our hearts, of course, and Rodney and me got into a right barney over the rights and wrongs of it all. I understood. You can't put a price on sentimental things like that, and it's never easy to let them go. As luck would have it though, I had the winning ticket, so the globe went straight back in the cabinet. Funny how things work out. I reckon it must have been God or something.

CASE STUDY #17

In 1980 we did a house clearance job over Deptford way. This old girl had passed on (she died), she had no family, and her landlord asked me to clear her place out. Up in the loft, among a few other bits and pieces, I found an old fob watch. All in all it was no prize catch. Hardly worth the effort really.

The Lesser Watch

Skip forward to 1996 and Raquel's mum and dad, James and Audrey, are coming over for dinner. It turns out James was in the antiques game, and I couldn't wait to chew his ear (I'd only recently got hold of a Jacobean cine-camera that I needed some advice on, so the timing was perfect). Anyway, that evening one drink led to another and we thought it best if James and Audrey stayed over the night, so Rodney stuck his motor in the garage. The next morning James came down to the garage to check on his wheels and it was then that something caught his eye in amongst all the bits and pieces of stock. It was that grubby old watch.

As it transpired, Jimbo's a bit of an expert on these things and he got so excited looking at this watch he had a hot flush and had to go and have a lay-down on the sofa. Sensing that this thing was worth a few quid I told Rodney to get the Cillit Bang out whilst I hunted about for a shammy leather, but Jimbo insisted we leave it to him. On his advice, and with his help, we put the watch into an auction (at Sotheby's, no less!). Well, it turns out that this grubby old watch was worth a bit more than we'd expected.

It ended up going for 6.2 million quid!

Shock ain't the word. I floated out of that auction in a state of numbness, the likes of which I hadn't felt since Bobby Moore lifted the World Cup. I can only imagine it's how Moses must have felt when he came down from Mount Cyanide. Now, a lot of people said that this was all a pure fluke, but I beg to differ. Yes, Rodney had pegged the watch for a worthless Victorian egg timer, but I'd obviously seen something in it that nobody else picked up on, otherwise I wouldn't have held on to it, would I? And granted, I did hold on to it for the best part of sixteen years before getting it valued, but when your schedule's as packed as mine was, you can't get round to ticking every little box.

The most important thing was that I'd finally done it. *We'd finally done it!*

We were *millionaires!**

---

* To be more precise, we'd been millionaires for sixteen years, we just didn't know it.

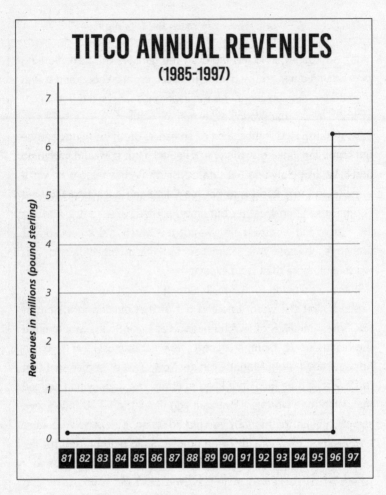

TITCO ANNUAL REVENUES
(1985-1997)

Revenues in millions (pound sterling)

81 82 83 84 85 86 87 88 89 90 91 92 93 94 95 96 97

1996 weren't a bad year.

Now, I've always been partial to a Nasdaq, and I'm a big fan of Wall Street (the film and the actual street itself), so with the coffers full it weren't long before I was seizing the opportunity to invest in the old futures market. You know me; I'm not one to rest on my laurels.

But here's the thing: when you reach the top, life has a funny way of doing its very best to knock you off your perch. You know by now that the world of business has a tendency to throw some surprises in your general direction. That's just the way the cookie bounces. You've gotta be very quick on your feet in this game. But there are times when not even Hussain Bolts can dodge what's coming. And when the South American financial market crashed, it was one of those times. We lost it all.

Then came the bankruptcy, which was an absolute travesty. I'd always paid my cheques on time, without fail. Fair enough, they bounced, but they were always on time. We ended up in debt to the tune of fifty grand! More's the point, we were skint! As if this wasn't enough, the courts then informed me that I was barred from running a company. It was like a knife to my soul, it really was. Telling Derek Trotter to stop running his own company is like telling David Beckham to stop playing with his balls. *Unthinkable!*

The one and only slither of good news amidst this sea of cock-ups was Nelson Mandela House. Being the shrewd operator that I am, I'd successfully sealed the purchase of the flat back in the early 1990s. What with the way the housing market was going I thought it'd be a good investment (and I weren't wrong). After flogging the watch, I'd put the flat up for sale but nobody wanted it (even with the carpet included). But most important of all, it was the only asset the company *didn't* own. Returning to the old place was like getting a much-needed hug, but that still didn't change the fact that we were in right lumber. My credit rating was so low I couldn't even pay with money! It looked as though TITCO was finished. Kaput. Dead. Dead as the emu.

But you know me well enough by now to know that Derek Trotter doesn't go down without a fight. No way, Pedro! I've always believed in the old adage that 'where there's a will there's a way'. Well, in this case it was 'where there's a *Rodney* there's a way'. Yes, I had been barred from running a company. But he hadn't. And so I did something I never thought I'd ever do: I made Rodney the new managing director of Trotters Independent Traders. I know what you're thinking: making Rodney the chairman of your board is like making Abu Hamza the captain of your volleyball team. And you're right. But what could I do?

And so I took a back seat, dealing with the little things like sales, acquisitions, wage distribution and overall strategy, and leaving Rodney to get on with the rest. Never one to play the blame game (even though it was Rodney's fault), I showed the mark of a great leader by accepting that mistakes had been made and taking it upon myself to fix them.

TITCO was alive and kicking again!

TITCO 2001. Rodney steps up to bat.

PART NINE

* * * * * * * * * * * * * * * * *

PERSONAL WELLBEING

★

Work hard, play harder. That was my outlook back in my younger days. Oh yes, with the right music and a few Tia Maria and Lucozades under my belt, no conga line was safe when I got on the floor. I was like Peckham's answer to Keith Moon. Rodney tried his best to keep up, bless him, but when it came to cutting loose beneath a glitter ball he was more Keith Harris than anything else. Of course I then met my Raquel, knocked out Damien, and I had to rein it in a bit. That's not to say I'm now a slippers and Hobnob man – you can still find me on the odd Saturday night doing the lambada at the Nag's Head disco – but I'm just that little bit more careful these days not to knock my pipe out.

DOWNTIME

All the top tycoons take their leisurely pursuits seriously. It might be something as simple as a round or two of golf or squash, or maybe baseball (there's nothing the successful yuppie likes more than whacking something around with a bat). Or it might be something a bit more 'out there'. Take Dickie Branston for example, who, when not running an airline or knocking about on Decker Island with Leonardo

Di Cappuccino, gets his kicks floating round the stratosphere in giant helium balloons. Not many people know this, but Deborah Meaden, the famous Dragon, opts for a bit of stock car racing when she needs to unwind.* Even fewer people know that Lord Alec Sugar has the biggest private collection of My Little Pony memorabilia in Europe.† And you can bet old Bill Gates likes to let loose – when he's not jetting back and forth from important summits on how best to limit the old carbon dioxide output. Having always been a man of action myself, I've tried many different activities over the years, from hang-gliding (a cinch!) to jet-skiing (always check your brakes are working before setting off).

A RIGHT RACKET

Back in the early nineties Rodney and I teamed up to play a few sets of badminton with Cassandra (always a sporty girl) and her boss, Stephen, at the bank's sports club. This was well after Rodney had punched Stephen on the nose and the fracture had since healed up nicely. I think the invitation was a gesture of goodwill to let us know there were no hard feelings. Perrier water under the bridge and all that.

As you can imagine, being the two top dogs on the court, the competition got a bit heated between Stephen and myself and there was plenty of good-natured sportsmanship-like ribbing. I regret it now but I did end up swinging for him at one point. We lost the match but that was mostly down to Rodney – he was all knees and elbows,

---

* This might not be, and probably isn't, true.
† This also might not be, and probably isn't, true.

staggering about the court like a pissed bloke trying to swat a wasp. Not that it bothered me that much. Whacking a dead budgie over a net is fun but after an hour or so it gets a bit boring.

Incidentally: the following week I received both a lifetime ban from the club and a bill for a new racket. I thought Stephen would have stepped in to smooth it all over but he wouldn't return any of my calls and when I went to see him at the bank he barricaded himself in the khazi and escaped through a ceiling panel. A proper David Copperfield job. But there you go. I never liked the bloke anyway. He was one of those ultra self-important types, you know, all Dallas and no oil. In short: a total banker. Unfortunately there're a lot of 'em about in this game.

Cassandra's former boss, Stephen. A total banker.

EXECUTIVE BURNOUT

Working in the old commodities market ain't all Beaujolais and Brie and cranberry tartlets. Oh no, it's a cut-throat, dog-eat-dog game we're in, and it can give you the massive hump. If you don't keep a handle on it, this can cause some serious long-term problems. Yes, stress can get to the best of us (even me!) and it's amazing how it can affect the body. The first time I became aware of the stress phenomenon was with my mate Denzil. He was always prone to bouts of worry and even sought professional help for it. In fact now that I think back, every time we did a bit of business together he'd end up in some sort of therapy.

In researching this book, I had the following telephone conversation with the man himself:

ME: *Denzil, me old mate. Tell me, when did you first become aware that you were feeling stressed?*

DENZIL: *When I answered the phone.*

ME: *No, I don't mean today. I mean when in your life?*

DENZIL: *Oh. It was probably during my teens. But it got worse as I got older.*

ME: *Did you find that your stress levels went through the roof after meeting Corinne?*

DENZIL: *Yeah, but that was only part of it. I don't know, I suppose I just always had this nagging sense of doom.*

ME: *I felt that way around her too.*

DENZIL: *I'm not talking about Corinne!*

ME: *Please explain.*

DENZIL: *Well ... don't take this the wrong way, Del, it's just ... how can I put this? Have you ever had the feeling that bad luck is following you around?*

ME: *What, you mean ... like a curse?*

DENZIL: *Exactly! Like a jinx.*

ME: *Yeah ... and?*

DENZIL: *And ... I always sort of had this feeling that ...*

ME: *That what?*

DENZIL: *That you were the jinx.*

ME: *Me?! Oh that's charming, that is! Thanks a lot, Denzil.*

DENZIL: *Don't be offended.*

ME: *Don't be offended? One of my oldest and bestest mates calls me a curse and I'm s'posed to just laugh it off?*

DENZIL: *Look, I'm not saying it's always completely your fault, but you've gotta admit when we hang around together things usually go wrong ... and I'm usually the one who gets the worst of it.*

ME: *What are you going on about, you tart?*

DENZIL: *All right, what about last year when you sold me that electric vape cigarette?*

ME: *There was nothing wrong with that vape.*

DENZIL: *Nothing wrong with it?! Del, it gave off so much vapour the entire street had to be evacuated! They could see it from the International Space Station!*

ME: *You just had it on the wrong setting, that's all.*

DENZIL: *And then there was the time back when we were at school and you dared me to poke that hornets' nest.*

ME: *That was your own fault for accepting the dare. There's always an element of risk involved in a dare, Denzil, that's why it's called a dare. Anyway, I'd never even heard of Hannah Filactic shock.*

DENZIL: *Del, I've gotta go ...*

ME: *What's the matter?*

DENZIL: *I'm hyperventilating ...*

ME: *That's all right, I can wait.*

[Muffled noises ('oh God, oh God!') inaudible ...]

ME: *Deep breaths, Denzil, deep breaths ... Denzil ...?*

My old mate, Denzil. Very trusting, very loyal and very stressed.

For Rodney it was even worse, though. I won't go into detail – it's all a bit embarrassing and really none of my business – but his lack of motivation ended up putting a bit of a strain on his marriage. Fortunately for me, stress just played havoc with my bowels (see page 221). Everything else remained in perfect working order. But this is why it's extra important to take some time out for yourself every now and then to relax and enjoy the fruits of your labour. Personally I've found that a few days in Benidorm or even a weekend fishing (avoid Cornwall) does the trick when I need to let off a bit of the old managerial steam. If you're really flush you could try the Grand Hotel in Brighton or the Hôtel de Paris in Monte Carlo.*

Most important of all, don't forget what really matters, those without whom it'd all be meaningless: your family and your mates. I mean, there's no point achieving your dreams if you've got nobody to share them with, is there?

STRESS MANAGEMENT

Make no mistake, the fast-paced high-pressured world of free enterprise is not for the faint of heart; making million-dollar decisions, staving off crashes and recessions (single *and* double-dip), keeping a close watch on both your domestic and overseas markets, sending emails, twittering, bloggering – no wonder so many of us have got the arse ache.

Thankfully with the rise in stress levels there has also been a rise in ways to tackle the issue head on. Most of today's top progressive

---

* A word of warning: for some reason they've got it in their heads that I owe them a monkey, so if you do go it's best not to mention me.

Rodney, channelling his inner Buddha.

firms take the mental health of their employees very seriously, with many offering their own 'wellbeing modules', which include everything from nap zones to ping-pong rooms. Some even go so far as replacing chairs with beanbags. Apparently it's all aimed at 'millennials' who prefer a more slack half-arsed work space. It's all very trendy and ostentatious, which suits me to a T (I've always been a bit millennial myself), but where do you draw the line? I'm all for less rigid, but beanbags is taking the piss. What next? Padded walls and free gripe water most probably.

That said, I am nothing if not forward-thinking (and let's face it, you can't whack a bit of ergonomics), so here're some other top alternative tips on how to battle work-based stress.

➲ 'ME' SPACES

A chance to grab a bit of peace and quiet in a frantic work environment can be a real lifesaver. We've always been a bit pushed for space here at the flat, so if Raquel's hoovering the bedroom I tend to opt for the balcony or the bog. If they're engaged, and Raquel is feeling particularly feisty, I have been known to head for the airing cupboard. At least it's warm in there.

➲ MEDITATION

Rodney and Cassandra were big on this at one point. As far as I can tell all you've gotta do is sit and breathe. A piece of cake!

➲ FENG SHUI

No, not raw fish (we'll get to that in a minute). Feng Shui, as Raquel explained to me, is when you create positive energy and harmony by moving your sofa around. We tried it once, got into a row and I ended up kipping on it. I blame the sofa. It always gave off a bad vibe.

That said, I reckon there's more to this ancient ergonomics lark than meets the eye. I mean, it makes sense that where you place things in a room is gonna have an impact on the time you spend in that room. Take our bathroom for instance, which has always been a very cold space, so much so that Albert once went so far as to suggest that it might be haunted. After explaining to him that no poltergeist in its right mind would choose to hang about in our bathroom, especially after he'd been in there (I'm tempted to say something about 'brown air situations' but I don't want to lower the overall tone), I pointed out the simple fact that the council had put the extractor fan in the wrong way round.

It just takes a bit of common sense, that's all, and while on first glance the flat might look like everything's just been dumped willy-nilly, nothing could be further from the truth. Being the multi-purpose space that it is, a lot of careful thought had to go into it.

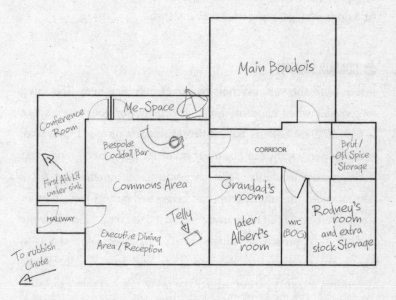

Notice how each zone is clearly designated, and yet at the same time the whole blends together effortlessly. Notice the uncluttered doorways and main thoroughfare, allowing for a safe and smooth to and fro of traffic. This is vital to the successful functioning of any work space, but it also applies to spaces in general. Pubs for example. Having patronised many the watering hole over the years, and being the observant type that I am, pub and bar ergonomics has become a bit of a speciality of mine. Take it from me, a wisely laid-out saloon (well-balanced table and chairs-to-standing-room ratio, ease of bog accessibility and/or a perfectly placed fruit machine) can make the world of difference. Call it nitpicking if you want, but that's just me, I'm a very discerning geezer. Far too many a good knees-up is ruined by a poorly lit basement khazi or a carelessly positioned dartboard. And don't even get me started on bar-flaps!

⊜ COLOUR SCHEME

Just as with the van, psychology comes into play here. The thing to consider when choosing a colour scheme for your work space is that different colours have different impacts on our brains and, when chosen wisely, can positively influence our general mood and decision-making ability. Most corporate environments opt for a neutral and calm palette: greys and beiges and pastel blues. In other words: dull. At TITCO I've always preferred to take a more dynamic and eclectic approach, allowing a broad plectrum of tints and hues to fight it out, meaning that your mood can, and does, rapidly change depending on what part of the flat you're staring at. From a distance it all melds into a kind of big browny-yellow mush, but up close it's an intense, hyper-real and eyeball-taxing experience designed to keep the energy high and the brain on full alert.* The closest synonymilie I can think of is a bomb going off in a Smarties factory.

---

* My original idea was to recreate the scheme for the front cover of this book, but the editor didn't want to run the risk of making people feel ill. And that is a very valid point worth mentioning. It's always best, if and when possible, not to make potential customers dry-heave.

⊘ FEELING A PRICK

Once a fortnight Denzil pays a Chinese sort to stick needles in his head. Sounds kinky, I know, but it's actually just an ancient form of alternative medicine known as 'acupuncture'. According to Denzil it's all about 'meridians' which are like streams of energy that flow through your body, and every once in a while these streams get clogged up. Whatever it is (Trigger reckons it's quantium physics, something to do with the Large Hardon Collider), it helps Denzil to relax and, even though I detect a strong whiff of bullshit, anything that helps a mate in need gets my full support.

Even so, you won't see Derek Trotter letting someone use him as a pin cushion any time soon. Meridian or no meridian, come at me with a needle and you are guaranteed at the very least a smack in the eye!

⊘ REGULAR EXERCISE

Apparently when you exercise the brain releases chemicals called endolphins, which are like nature's Prozac. I've got my doubts on this one. Considering how often the lifts in Nelson Mandela House have been out of action, you'd have thought Rodney would have had endolphins coming out of his ears by now.

⊘ LAST BUT NOT LEAST ...

If you've got a van, kick it!

NUTRITION

I used to think that food was for wimps. Back in the eighties, blokes like me (yuppies) rarely had time to sit down, let alone eat a meal. I was living life on the edge, nerves on red alert, fuelled only by a beta blocker and a dream, so I tended to eat on the go – mobile phone in one hand, Pot Noodle in the other. Of course there was the odd power lunch with a client here and there, usually something light (a mutton tikka madras, the occasional Whopper, that sort of thing), but other than that I was too busy walking the yuppie tightrope to worry about little things like hunger. I then met Raquel and have since become much more esoteric when it comes to all things diet. You see, just as

Me, eating some fruit, circa 1983.

it's very important to put the right petrol in your motor, it's also vital that you put the right food down your gullet. So I'm now going to share with you some tips that I guarantee will keep both the engine ticking over and, more importantly, *you* on top of your business game!

Now, I'm no Gillian McKeith (there ain't rubber gloves thick enough to get me sifting through the Eartha Kitts the way that poor cow does) but I have learned a few things. For example, did you know that nuts are an excellent source of energy? I didn't either until quite recently, but it makes sense when you think about it (when was the last time you saw a knackered squirrel?). And that's why these days I like to make sure I'm never too far from a packet of dry roasted. Oily fish is very good for you too, so don't forget to top up on the scampi every once in a while.

On the subject of fish, if you've got a lunch date with an important client coming up and you *really* want to impress (and you've got an iron stomach and a strong gag reflex), try sushi. And before you say '*But that's raw fish, Del!*' yes, I know! I'm not a wally, am I? But think about it this way: 4.2 billion Chinese people can't be wrong, can they? A word of warning though: if you're aiming to knock the socks off some sort, make sure you've got an emergency box of Tic Tacs handy. I speak from experience here – during her pregnancy Raquel's hormones were up the wall and she went mad for tuna. It reached the point where saying goodnight to her was like snogging Moby Dick.

★ **DON'T SKIP BREAKFAST – I DID ONCE BACK IN 1979 AND IT WAS BLOODY 'ORRIBLE!** ★

Sid. He was no Nigella Lawson.

VENUES AND TABLE MANNERS

So you've lined up a potential player in your next earth-shuddering business venture and you want to sweeten things up and seal the deal. A slap-up meal is in order. But where to book?

It really depends on the client. Up in Sloane Square they go mad for a roasted pepper and a bucket of couscous. Where I'm from it's more of a sausage roll and a tattoo crowd. If it's Trigger, a pint of bitter and a cheese roll usually does the trick. There's no right or wrong in it really, just different horses for different courses.

Whenever I weren't in the mood for the Dorchester or I was getting bored with the Ivy, I'd usually pop down to my local cafe, the 'Fatty Thumb'. I ate there most days for nigh on thirty years, so Sid, the owner, knew exactly how to cater to my personal culinary requirements. Sid is what I'd call 'old school' and so never really went a bundle on what he refers to as 'poncey grub'. Then again, Sid's never been that cultured (he thought couscous played up-front for Hungary). And this was very much reflected in his establishment, which was all grease, sticky seats and coughing. Not a krudite in sight! But as Sid so often pointed out, with a warm glimmer of pride in his eyes, he'd only been closed down *four* times. At the end of the day – and the occasional bout of amoebic dysentery aside – the grub weren't that bad (just as long as you avoided the porridge: the one and only time Rodney ordered a bowl he was up all night coughing up fur-balls).

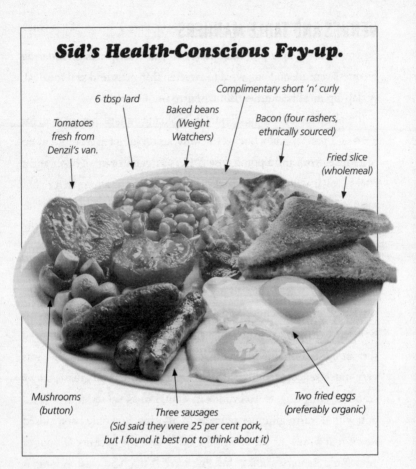

Sid's Health-Conscious Fry-up.

Tomatoes
fresh from
Denzil's van.

6 tbsp lard

Baked beans
(Weight
Watchers)

Complimentary short 'n' curly

Bacon (four rashers,
ethnically sourced)

Fried slice
(wholemeal)

Mushrooms
(button)

Three sausages
(Sid said they were 25 per cent pork,
but I found it best not to think about it)

Two fried eggs
(preferably organic)

If you do decide to go upmarket, you may well find it all a bit daunting. Some of these top-class restaurants follow strict rules and have very high standards when it comes to both serving up and eating the old haute cuisine. Trust me, it's a minefield out there and what should be a relaxing and joyful experience can all too often feel like a *Krypton Factor* assault course of booby-traps and zip-wires that only the very shrewdest and sophisticated of diners can navigate.

HERE'RE A FEW POINTERS TO AVOID LOOKING LIKE A TOTAL PHILISTINE:

- Don't click your fingers to get the waiter's attention. It's considered rude. A short, sharp 'Oi!' or 'John!' will suffice.

- If there's a bowl of water with a slice of lemon in it on the table, it's for dipping your fingers in, *not* drinking.

- Testing the wine. Always a crucial moment in separating the refined from the rabble, drinking wine is an art form in itself. So when the bottle arrives, let it be known that you know the difference between your table wine and your *vin ordinaire*. If you're asked to test the cork, *don't* sniff it. A quick suck and a 'pour on, McDougal' is all that's needed. When it comes to testing the 'bouquet', I always follow the 'four-S' rule: *swirl, sniff, swig and spit*. Just make sure you've got an extra glass to gob it out into.

★   *SWIRL + SNIFF + SWIG + SPIT = AN ALL-ROUND CLASS ACT!*   ★

- Be very careful when there are lit candles on the table – especially important if you're wearing a tie or sporting a beard. One Christmas Uncle Albert reached for a cracker and came very close to spontaneously combusting.

- If at any point you feel a belch coming on, either do it quietly and swallow it, or offer the table a polite 'excuse me, I'm just going to the bog'.

- Remember: it's not a race, so eat slowly and give enough time between each mouthful to allow for a natural and civilised exchange of ideas. Aim for the two-ideas-per-mouthful mark and you'll be laughing.

- Keep the conservation on cultured and tasteful topics only. Nobody wants to hear about the last time you had your lugholes syringed when they've got a mouthful of muse-boosh.

- Gentlemen: always make sure to tuck your serviette securely into your collar.

- Ladies: there's nothing at all wrong with showing a bit of chest, but there's also nothing more off-putting than a cleavage full of peas.

- If you do drop a bit of food on the floor (dumplings can be a bugger), don't just pick it up and eat it. Make sure you blow any bits of debris off first.

- Tip generously. Nobody likes a tight-wad.

- I've always felt that a simple 'please give my condiments to the chef' is a nice way to go out.

RODNEY AND OTHER VEGETABLES

Being the hot-blooded alpha male that I am, I've never really taken much to veg. I love a dollop of mash with my pie and a Brussels sprout at Christmas is a must, but I've always been more partial to a bit of stodge. Rodney, on the other hand, is what is known as an 'occasional vegetarian', which I think goes a long way in explaining his overall low-energy approach to life. (One time he even claimed to be a vegan – I dunno, must have been all that *Star Trek* he watched as a nipper.)

Basically every couple of years or so he sees a documentary about the rainforest, hosted by Geldof, Sting, Boneo or one of that mob, and he gets a sudden surge of social conscience and decides he's going to save the planet by eating cabbage. This normally lasts about a fortnight before the depression sets in and he goes out on a cow binge. As I've repeatedly said to him, if God meant us to live off vegetables why did He create the kebab? It just goes in one ear and out the other. But then as my dear old mum used to say, 'There's none so blind as them what won't listen.'

Authentic British grub. The kebab!

Me, contemplating a bowl of roughage, circa 1989.

WARNING!

Back in the late eighties I started to get a bit of Cynthia (pain) in the old New Delhi (belly). At first I brushed it off. *Probably just a stray meat samosa lodged in the lower intestines*, I thought. I tried everything: Andrews Liver Salts, Campari and prune juice, burping, but the pain just got worse. I ended up in hospital where the quacks were just as confused as I was as to the cause. I don't mind admitting I was a bit scared. I weren't throwing a paddy or nothing, but still, up till then I'd never really had anything wrong with me, so I couldn't help but worry. At one point I even overheard a couple of nurses mention the words 'terminal illness', which just added to my fear and confusion. I mean, I'd come over a bit nauseous at a bus depot once, but that's about it. To make matters worse, Rodney then suggested a CAT scan. I couldn't believe it! There I was in the middle of a gastric meltdown, the arse about to fall out of my world, and that plonker wanted to get the vets involved!

Anyway, after the umpteenth test was completed, it turned out that I was suffering from an irritable bowel syndrome. The doctor told me it was brought on primarily by stress and that it was a common ailment among yuppies. Well, that made perfect sense (the real mystery is why my bowel hadn't been irritated *sooner*!) Another factor was poor diet, fried food and takeaways. All in all it was a very uncomfortable lesson in the importance of roughage.

TOP TIP!

★

EAT PLENTY OF MUESLI AND TRY TO GIVE YOUR GUTS A GOOD CLEAR-OUT AT LEAST TWICE A DAY.

★

PART TEN
★★★★★★★★★★★★★

ETHICS

★

o, I'm not talking about model airplanes. I'm talking about values and integrity. Now, I'll be the first to admit that I haven't always done everything strictly above board (which wouldn't be the case if the board didn't keep shoving me down), but as Raquel says, my heart's in the right place. I mean, I've always done my best by my family; I've never dealt in drugs or guns or things that hurt people, and every Christmas, without fail, I've gone round the estate to see to it that the old folks are all right for a bit of company, a mince pie and a giggle. And this gentle and compassionate approach is something that has always crossed over into my business dealings. The little white lies aside, it's vital that you be honest and upfront with people and make sure that whatever you do it has a positive impact on those around you. Just remember what that cricket thing in *Pinocchio* said: 'If you're ever in doubt, listen to your conscience.'

Spreading the festive joy. Me in the market, circa 1982.

CASE STUDY #18

Back in the mid eighties I found myself coming face to face with a depressed rhinoceros. No, I hadn't been sniffing the Pritt Stick, I'm serious. You see, a contact of mine owned a private zoo over Dulwich way, and he was letting it be known that he had a rhino going cheap. I was curious (who wouldn't be?) so I booked myself a viewing. As blown away as I was when I clapped eyes on the rhino, I could also see why he wanted it shifting. It was well past its prime (at least late fifties) and spent most of its time kipping.

Still, my mind was a whirlpool of possibilities and I was certain that with my guidance I could at the very least get it a bit of television work (an area in which to this day rhinos are still sadly under-represented). Oh yes, with me at its side there'd have been no stopping us. It would've been the Kanoo Reeves of the rhino world, the biggest thing since Lassie croaked.

Sensing my enthusiasm, the owner immediately began talking figures. But as I stood there staring at the big grey mass of wrinkles snoring away in the hay, it suddenly opened its eyes and looked back at me. I don't know what it was (maybe it was Mum, maybe it was Jesus), but in that moment, as man and beast shared a silent gaze,

Late fifties and cream-crackered. Definitely the saddest rhino I've ever seen.

I snapped back to my senses. Well, I'd have never got it in the van anyway. And what would the neighbours have said? On top of that I could just picture Rodney taking it for walkies over the park. I washed my hands of the whole thing right there and then and that was the end of it.

Or so I thought. You see, over the next few days I couldn't get that look out of my head. They were definitely the saddest rhino eyes I'd ever seen. Truth be told, I felt sorry for the poor cock. I mean, there he was, out of his natural habitat, trapped and fed up. Looking back now I think I saw a bit of myself in him – I don't mean looks-wise, he was an ugly-looking sod – I just mean it, you know, metaphysically. It got so bad that it was keeping me awake at night, as if some weird telescopic connection had been formed – every time I closed my eyes I saw *those* eyes, calling to me, pleading: *Help me, Del, I don't belong here, I belong in the jungle with all the other rhinocerosesses*.

At one point I was even considering breaking into the zoo and setting it free. It would've been at least a three-man job by my reckoning. I could've relied on Trigger, and Monkey Harris (a natural when it came to cracking a Chubb) could've been persuaded. But then I would've needed some serious transport. Denzil had his lorry but Corinne was on the warpath at the time and being a rhino's getaway driver was the last thing he needed.

It all ended up being epidemic anyway, as a few weeks later I received the sad news that the rhino was on its way out. I went to visit it one last time, took it a Scotch egg, and said *bonjour*. As emotional as it was, that night I slept like a baby, guilt-free and assured in the knowledge that I'd done right by one of God's ugliest and most misunderstood of creatures.

Amen.

GIVING BACK

When you're a successful captain of industry, navigating the fiscal swells as you scour the horizon for opportunity, it can be very easy to lose sight of where you've come from. In this game, you've gotta go where the readies take you, and in my time they took me all over the planet. But as much as it was nice to see the world and soak up new culture, I must admit there was always a small part of me that pined for Peckham: this ancient metropolis, its people (most of whom I can call acquaintances, many I call friends), the cut and thrust of the busy marketplace, the pie and mash and the pollution. It's in my blood. And that's why I've always felt it important to give something back to the community. Whether it's helping to fit a new roof for the church, rebuilding the local hospice, disposing of a deceased gypsy's ashes to help out a grieving mate, or just looking out for the welfare of Sikh bikers, nothing quite gives me the warm sense of satisfaction that doing a good deed does.

THINK ENVIRONMENTALLY

Thanks to Damien, 'green thinking' has very much become part of TITCO's core culture over the last decade or so. He claims he did it just to shut Rodney up, but I know that deep down he cares (heart of gold, that boy).

I'll be honest, this sort of thing never used to bother me that much. I was always too busy trying to earn an honest crust, keep my nose clean and put the groceries in the fridge to worry about holes in o-zones, leaded fuel, bi-polar ice-caps, and what 'ave yer. But then I grew up in 1950s London, so I've always felt right at home in a cloud of smog.

Actually it's frightening to think of it now – I must have more lead in me than a butcher's pencil! Back then, though, the weather was just weather. Nowadays we've got global warming to worry about. And worry I do. I can't tell you how many sleepless nights I've had thinking about longer summers, rising sea waters, homeless polar bears and O2 omissions. It can get a bit depressing so I try my best to look on the bright side. I mean, at least when we come to sell the flat again we'll be able to advertise it as having sea views. And polar bears can swim. They could always emigrate to Scotland or somewhere like that.

'*But what can my business do to help reduce greenhouse gases, Del?*' I hear you say.

Me and Damien soaking up a spot of global warming in the south of France, circa 2001.

THANKFULLY, THERE'RE LOTS OF LITTLE THINGS YOU CAN DO ...

- First and foremost, get shot of your greenhouse. We've only got a shed on the allotment. It's never smelled too clever but it ain't giving off any gases as far as I know.

- Cut down on your fossil fuels. We're on gas here at the flat so this ain't a problem for us.

- Recycle. For years now I've been putting my paper, glass and plastic waste into separate bin liners. Bung 'em all down the chute and bish-bash-bosh! Job done!

- Drive less. Not only is walking and cycling very good exercise, it also reduces your old carbon footprint. Just make sure you've got a padlock for your bike and keep an eye out for muggers.

- Make efficiency goals. Get ideas from your staff on this and treat them when goals are met. They're much more likely to embrace your initiative if you get them involved and make it as fun as possible. If they don't, threaten them with the sack and give them an official warning. Making things fun is all well and good but don't let 'em take the piss.

- Serve sustainable brain grub at meetings: nuts, fruits, scampi etc.

- Think before you flush. Did you know that the average Brit flushes the toilet five times a day and that older bogs can use up to nine litres of water per flush? Well, you do now. The fact is that toilet flushing is the largest single use of a household's water consumption. Makes you think, don't it? Thankfully if you can just hold on a bit longer you can save gallons of water every day. Just think how much you'd save in a year! This was a frequent problem with Rodney, who's always had a weak bladder, especially when he's nervous, which is most of the time. Of course back when Grandad and Uncle Albert were still with us you needed as much water in your flush as you could get. Gordon Bennett, there were jet hoses not powerful enough for that job.

Never one to miss a trend (see page 167), when global warming kicked off I made sure to get in on the ground floor. That might sound a bit cynical, but let's face it, saving the Earth is big business and only a dipstick of the 42-carat variety wouldn't want a piece of that pie. Look at that Alf Gore geezer (very much the Don Cannelloni of all things global and warming); he can't even step onto his private jet without tripping over a wad of bunse. But it's not just the luxury jet, the twenty-roomed villa and the joy of having Barbra Streisand pop round for a supper of endangered species on toast that matters. The most important thing is that he's doing his bit for the planet, and saving humanity from a very moist and humid demise in the process. And in that sense we're very much alike, Alf and me.

CASE STUDY #19

Back in the early noughties I looked into acquiring my very own wind turbine – the *bonnet de douche* in alternative cost-free energy technology. Now, I don't know if you've noticed, but most of these turbines are stuck out at sea or in the middle of fields where no one lives. What's the point in that? I wanted to get one fitted in over by the pram sheds. I had no intention of stinting on the wattage either; I wanted something big enough to power the entire estate. Easier said than done, though. I put word about that I was in the market for a turbine, but drew a blank. Next I wrote to the council but they were too busy mugging motorists to even bother to write back.

Then I had a brainwave: if I couldn't get one big one, why not have loads of little ones? Damien and I went about testing the idea by setting up fifty electric fans on the balcony and then hooking them up to a generator. Then it was just a simple case of sitting back and waiting for some wind. When that didn't arrive, Damien tried to create some of his own wind by plugging a load more fans into the mains (as much as I'm proud of him, there are times I despair of that boy). We gave the wind one more chance, then three weeks later a very slight and gentle breeze put in an appearance. Bottom line: I'd created more energy the last time I blew my nose. But that's all right. When it comes to the science of saving us all from certain doom, trial and error is the name of the game, innit?

INCLUSIVITY

I couldn't write a book like this without touching upon this sensitive but very important subject. And so, ever cautious not to offend, I made sure I did a bit of research first on the old Google and double-checked my dictionary, just to be safe. The whole process was a real eye-opener.

If, like me, you're getting on in years, you'll probably agree that things were a lot simpler and clearer back in the day. I mean, back when I was growing up, a bloke was a bloke and a bird was a bird. You knew where you stood. Not that I've got anything at all against the LWT community (a smashing bunch of lads), but it can't half get confusing sometimes. You see, in this day and age nothing is quite what it seems and identity is king (or queen) (or other). To put it very simply: some birds are bees and some bees are birds, some are half-bird-half-bee, some are the spirits of birds or bees, and others would get the serious hump if you referred to them as either a bird or a bee.

The first real inkling I got of this phenomenon was back in the early 1980s when Rodney and I were at a nightclub and, on his urging, I attempted to chat up a couple of sorts sitting at the bar. There I was, Caribbean Stallion in hand, the charm laser beams cranked up to eleven, thinking I was about to pull a couple of ravers, when I discovered they were in fact a couple of geezers. It was a minor shock to the system, but nothing I couldn't handle. The same can't be said for Rodney, who, still very wet behind the ears at the time, started sucking his thumb and drifting off to a happy place. Then again, that was nothing compared to Grandad, who spat his tea out and had to go and have a lay down when Boy George first appeared on *Top of the Pops*.

But like I said, they were different times back then. Apparently the medical term for all this is 'gender diphtheria'. It brings to mind Trigger's cousin, Ronnie. He was always a bit different from the rest of the lads, most obviously in his taste in women (they were men). I saw him only last week in Sainsbury's. Dressed to the nines he was: blouse, stockings, miniskirt, high-vis vest, five o'clock shadow and a beer gut. But at the end of the day, if he's happy, that's all that matters. Good for you, Ronnie, I say. Don't let the bastards drag you down!

Modern business is all about inclusivity and diversity, which is just as well 'cos as far as I'm concerned it can't be whacked. I've got mates who are Chinese, Jamaican, Ugandan, Nigerian, Bangladeshi ... even Welsh! You should have been at the Nag's Head for my sixtieth birthday bash – it was like a meeting of the United Nations, just more pissed. And this is something that has always crossed over into my approach to business: black, white, rich, poor, male, female, translingual, straight, gay-but-curious, mildly homoerogenous or full-blown Christopher Biggins – you could have four arms and your head on back to front for all I care – trivial little differences are meaningless, especially when there's a bit of bunse on the table.

WARNING!

I've never been one to beat around any bushes. When I see a dipstick I call that dipstick a dipstick. 'Honesty's always the best policy,' my mum used to say, and that's a rule I've lived my life by. Even when I tell the occasional and unavoidable little porky pie, I at least tell it honestly.

Under ordinary circumstances I'd advise anyone to take the same approach, but in this day and age circumstances are anything but ordinary. You see, we are living in very fragile and sensitive times; people are feeling a lot more feelings and the general feeling is that those feelings must be protected. Or to put it another way: the tarts have taken over the cockpit and they're copping the needle all over the shop! And that is why words are very dangerous these days and you can get into a lot of trouble for saying the wrong ones. This being the case, you have to be very careful with your words, how you say them and who you say them to, 'cos one wrong turn of phrase or carelessly uttered opinion could very well see you getting your collar felt. Of course, I ain't saying that freedom of speech has been flushed down the kermit; this great nation of ours was built on the wonderful cornerstone that is the Rule of Law, and to suggest otherwise would be ridiculous! No, the fact is that you can say whatever you want and whenever and however you want to say it – just as long as you don't upset the wrong people. You might well be thinking: '*Steady on, Del, have you been puffing on one of Rodney's Moroccan Woodbines?*' But I ain't joking.* And as if all this ain't enough to worry about, there are even things now called 'micro-aggressions' (similar to normal aggressions but much smaller and less aggressive). According to the article Damien showed me, I commit at least ten of these micro-aggressions every morning before I've even finished my Weetabix! But that's the thing – such is their microscopic nature they're very difficult to spot. If you think you might be doing this or you don't think that you are but you ain't 100 per cent certain if you are or you ain't ... pack it in!

---

* Jokes are a big 'no-no' n' all.

Bottom line: we live in the era of the 'ism'. *What's an 'ism' Del?* you're most probably wondering. Well, the better question would be: What *ain't* an 'ism'? We've got racism, sexism, homophobism, chauvinism, ageism, ableism, classism, pwonounciationism, antiterrorism, metabolism, photojournalism ... the list is endless!

And that brings me neatly on to another wonderful 'ism' to impact the modern age we call ... now.

FEMINISM

Back when I founded TITCO, feminism was just a harmless rumour. It was the sort of thing you thought only happened to other people, like Morris dancing or being hit by lightning. These days it's not only much more in your face, it's actually taken seriously.

Thankfully I've had Raquel fill me in on all the dos and do nots of the cause. She's always had a bit of a militant streak when it comes to these things. Don't get me wrong, she's not one of those *morbidly* feminist sorts, she just cares.

I'll be honest, most of the time I just switch off, grin and nod my head when she gives one of her 'talks'. To do otherwise just ain't worth the headache (she might look like a sweet and comely angel but get her going and she turns into a bloodthirsty banshee from hell – albeit an attractive and loveable one). But that's not to say that the odd word or two doesn't sink in.

Apparently there's this thing now called 'toxic masculinity' which basically means those ultra-macho chauvinistic types of men. I can vouch for this as I've come across plenty of cavemen in my time – the sort of blokes who think a woman's place is at the ironing board or in the kitchen making a sandwich – you know the type. And that's why I have always made a point of taking a woman's feelings into consideration. It just takes a bit of care, that's all. It's so easy to hurt a woman deeply with a thoughtless word or a badly timed gesture, and I'm not just talking about the good-looking ones, I mean the bow-wows too. I also make sure that I do my fair share of the housework. I don't go mad – hoovering and dusting have never been my strong suits – but I always help make the bed. Well, I get out of it.

And while Raquel (who funnily enough enjoys ironing and makes a blinding sandwich) does cop the hump from time to time, I balance the mood-o-meter by taking her out once a fortnight to Nando's. Every woman deserves a splash of glamour in her life once in a while and nothing melts the anger away like half a chicken Perry-Perry and a mixed-leaf salad. Lovely jubbly!

Love at first sight. Me and Raquel getting cozy on the chaise lounge, circa 1988.

As part of my research for this book, I set up the dictaphone, donned a crash helmet, and conducted a little one-on-one with Raquel:

ME: *Raquel, dear heart, love of my life, soulmate of my dreams, what's this feminism lark all about?*

RAQUEL: *Feminism is a cause that fights for the right for women to be treated equally.*

ME: *Equally to who?*

RAQUEL: *To men.*

ME: *Makes sense. So why do they burn their bras?*

RAQUEL: *They don't. Well, some might have, back in the 1960s, but they don't any more.*

ME: *Maybe they were itchy.*

RAQUEL: *What were itchy?*

ME: *The bras. I mean, bra technology has come on a bundle in the last half century. Some now even come with a high-tech foam padding that has its own memory. A bit like a Tempur mattress, but for boobs.*

RAQUEL: *Del, it had nothing to do with itchiness or inferior padding. It was a symbolic statement about liberation from male oppression.*

ME: *Yeah, of course, I was just saying ... you know ... bras must be a lot more comfy nowadays. 'Ere, did I ever tell you about my old mate, Nipper Hollins? He set fire to an entire wardrobe once. Then again, he* *never was working with a full deck. He was what psychiatrists call a styromaniac.*

RAQUEL: *A pyromaniac.*

ME: *Yeah, one of them 'n' all, most probably. So, what feminists are saying is that they want women to be treated the same as men?*

RAQUEL: *Yes, in a nutshell.*

ME: *Right, but if I treated you the way I treat, say, Boycie, for example, you'd do your pieces. And rightly so.*

RAQUEL: *Yes, but when I say 'equal treatment to men' I don't mean you should squirt onion purée in my hair conditioner or ask me to pull your finger. I'm talking about equal footing and representation. There's nothing a man can do that a woman can't do equally well.*

ME: *Oh, I'm all for that. 'She who dares wins', that is my motto. Some of the toughest people I know have been women. My dear old mum for one. Then there's Marlene and Cassandra ... and you, of course. You've always been a woman.*

RAQUEL: *Yes. Thank you.*

ME: *Do you remember when you gave birth to Damien?*

RAQUEL: *I have a vague recollection.*

ME: *It was probably all that gas and air. I remember it like it was yesterday. Especially when I first saw his head poking out, his little face all screwed up and covered in gunk, you screaming like that thing out of* The Exorcist.

RAQUEL: *You have such a way with words.*

ME: *Yeah, it's no wonder I ended up writing books. One more question: should feminism play any role in the workplace?*

RAQUEL: *Of course it should!*

ME: *Yeah ... I know ... I was just testing you. Anyway, that should be enough. I appreciate it, sweetheart. And as a way of saying thank you I am now going to give Nando's a bell, get them to reserve our special table for Friday night. I know I've got my faults, but you ain't done too badly, have yer?*

RAQUEL: *It could have been worse.*

ME: *Yeah. Right, I'll let you get back to the ironing.*

RAQUEL: *Thanks.*

Now, I could write a whole book about feminism (and one day I probably will), but for the time being I'll leave you with two simple pointers that should see you all right:

1. Do not, under any circumstances whatsoever, smack a woman on the bum and ask her if she fancies a curry. No matter how much you think it'll impress, the very strong likelihood is she won't appreciate it.

2. If you're ever in doubt, just remember: women are people too.

My soulmate, Raquel, circa 1990.

PART ELEVEN

★★★★★★★★★★★★★★★★★★★★★★★

GETTING TO KNOW ME

★

You've got this far, all the bases and potential pitfalls have been covered, but you might still be thinking to yourself: '*Who is the real Derek Trotter and what makes him tick? If only I could get half an hour of his time to chew his ear.*' You'd most probably want to sit me down for a bit of a Q&A. Well, you can't. Time is money and mine is precious, I'm afraid. But if you could, it would probably go something like this:

YOU: *So, what are you working on at the moment?*

ME: *A screenplay called* Dracula on the Moon. *I'd rather not say what it's about at this point.*

YOU: *When were you at your happiest?*

ME: *When my son, Damien, was born. Best thing that happened to me since my mum died. Raquel, my significant other, went through hell squeezing him out, but it was well worth the stitches.*

YOU: *What are your greatest fears?*

ME: *Doctors and Old Bill.*

YOU: *What is your earliest memory?*

ME: *My mum rocking me to sleep, singing a lullaby between puffs on a Woodbine.*

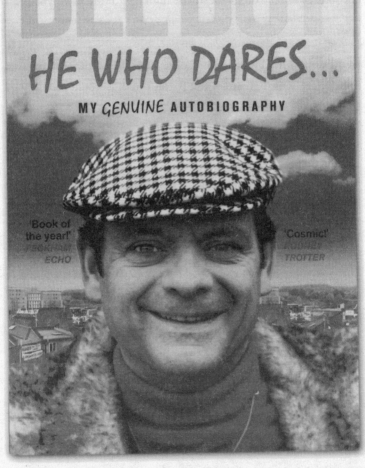

My favourite book. My autobiography, He Who Dares.

YOU: *What do you most dislike about yourself?*

ME: *My bowel. It gives me gyp.*

YOU: *Who has been your greatest influence?*

ME: *My mum. It's from her that I got my strong work ethic and sense of refinement. Michael Douglas would come a close second.*

YOU: *What is your most treasured possession?*

ME: *The award for bravery I got back in 1996 from the Mayor of Peckham. I singlehandedly apprehended a gang of muggers. It was nothing really, just doing my volvic duty.*

YOU: *What trait do you most deplore in others?*

ME: *Tightness. Take my mate Boycie, for example. He's so tight, he's the sort of bloke who buys a tin of baked beans on Tuesday just so he can have a bubble bath on Wednesday.*

YOU: *What do you most dislike about your appearance?*

ME: *Nothing.*

YOU: *What is your favourite book?*

ME: *My autobiography,* He Who Dares, *which is available online and in all good bookshops. It's got everything you could want from a book: suspense, violence, a car chase and a good dollop of Humpty-Dumpty.*

YOU: *I heard that it made the* Sunday Times *bestseller list.*

ME: *Yeah, well … it was nothing really.*

YOU: *I enjoyed it immensely. It was both exhilarating and enlightening. All in all it is probably the best book I've ever read. Thank you for writing it.*

ME: Mais ouis, mais ouis. *The great British book-reading public know a classic when they spot one. That's all there is to say about it really.*

YOU: *You must be very proud.*

ME: *Oh, the whole experience was* bonnet de douche.

YOU: *What about this book?*

ME: *Well, yeah, this one's pukka 'n' all. Plus it's red.*

YOU: *What is your favourite film?*

ME: Wall Street. *It changed my life.*

YOU: *Your favourite song?*

ME: *'Old Shep'. As songs about dead dogs go, it's 42-carat!*

YOU: *What's your favourite poem?*

ME: *'If' by Kipling. I love his cakes too. Very talented man.*

YOU: *And your favourite meal?*

ME: *A mutton madras at the Star of Bengal, Peckham. The owner, Tony, knows just how I like it.*

YOU: *Who would you most like to come to dinner?*

ME: *Gandhi. I'd ask him how he remained so calm and focused in the face of massive adversity. Plus I've got a box of men's wigs in the garage and I know I could find something in there that'd do his bonce up a treat. If Gandhi couldn't make it I'd go for Fiona Bruce.*

YOU: *Do you believe in aliens?*

ME: *No, but my mate Trigger does. According to him they turn up in the small hours every Thursday and move his bins around. I keep telling him it's probably the bin men but he won't have it.*

YOU: *What is your guilty pleasure?*

ME: *Gambling, alcohol and curry. But I don't feel guilty.*

YOU: *What is one thing that people might not know about you?*

Gandhi.   *Fiona Bruce.*

ME: *I'm very sentimental. I cried when Bambi's mum died. Boycie cheered.*

YOU: *What would you like your headstone to say?*

ME: *'Here lies Derek Trotter, a man of class, a man of principle, a man who made a difference. Brown bread but never forgotten. Bonsoir.' Something simple and understated like that.*

YOU: *Where do you find inspiration?*

ME: *I often get asked this. It can get a bit annoying sometimes. But the truth is that I've never had to look too far for it. There have been times when I've felt inspired just looking at myself in the mirror while having a shave. But if ever I'm feeling a touch deflated after a long hard day in the city, a bit of classical music is usually enough to rekindle the spirits: the theme tune to the Old Spice advert, Beethoven, Viverdi, a bit of Chas and Dave, that sort of thing. Other times I'll watch an uplifting film like* Kevin Brockovich, *or maybe a dark comedy like* The Elephant Man. *But mostly I find inspiration in the simple everyday things: the sight of a misty Peckham dawn; the sun's rays fighting to pierce the diesel fumes rising off the Old Kent Road; the laughter of children as they chuck rocks at the burnt-out Fiat Punto carcass over by the pram sheds; the little whistling sound coming from Raquel's nostrils when she sleeps, and the way those nostrils flare when she's gearing up to tackle another pile of ironing. Or it could be the smell of old banknotes (not those 'orrible new plastic ones), wafting up out of a full and well broken-in wallet.*

YOU: *It's been an absolute pleasure talking to you.*

ME: *I know.* Bonjour.

A DAY IN MY LIFE

I've never been one to keep a diary. I've always been too busy. But that ain't to say I don't take mental notes. That's what this book is – a lifetime's worth of mental notes. Given the opportunity, though, I bet you wouldn't mind being a fly on my shoulder for the day. Of course, it could never happen; there ain't no flies on me, never have been, never will be. But speaking purely hypnothetically, if you *were* perched on my shoulder for twenty-four hours, a typical and randomly chosen day in the life of Del Trotter would have gone something like this:

7.00 a.m. Get up, shower, shave, clean teeth, splash of Brut. (Unless I'd had a particularly heavy one the night before down the One-Eleven club or a dodgy mutton vindaloo at the Star of Bengal. Then there'd be no telling what time I'd get up. Sometimes I ended up just kipping in the bog.)

7.30 a.m. Breakfast: one boiled egg, runny. Wholewheat soldiers. Freshly squeezed grapefruit juice. Tea (skimmed milk). Raquel's on the cholesterol warpath again so I'm on my best behaviour.

7.45 a.m. Browse papers (*Peckham Echo*, *Exchange and Mart*, *Financial Times*, in that order). Always good to keep up to date with world events and see what the markets are up to.

8.00 a.m. Raquel takes on a fresh pile of laundry. She loves a bit of ironing, that girl.

8.30 a.m. Rodney emerges. Too hungover for breakfast. Starts banging on about the state of the rainforest. I tune it out by catching up on my correspondence: two letters. Both final demands.

9.00 a.m. Raquel starts doing a bit of aggressive hoovering, which signals that it's time for me to make myself scarce.

9.30 a.m. Pitch up at market. Today's stock: genuine full-scale reprints of Michael Angela's 'The Last Dinner'. Rodney showing signs of stress.

11.15 a.m. Slow day. Punters ain't biting. Rodney's fallen asleep.

11.45 a.m. Trigger passes on his rounds. First sale of the day.

A spot of inspirational reading before my nightcap.

12.00 p.m. Sid's Café. Sausage, egg, bacon, mushrooms, beans, fried slice, Kit-Kat. Four cups of tea.

12.45 p.m. Auction house. Put in winning bids for a consignment of near-perfect, genuine antique Edwardian carriage clocks (batteries not included) and an autographed poster of Kriss Akabusi.

1.15 p.m. Nag's Head Public House. Celebrate: One sausage sandwich, mustard, red *and* brown sauce, two packets of salt and vinegar crisps, four pina coladas and two Drambuie and Diet Cokes. Non-alcoholic lager tops for Rodney (he's driving).

6.30 p.m. Home. Raquel slams dinner on table: poached salmon, new potatoes, salad. Can't stomach it. Think I'm coming down with a touch of yuppie flu. Reckon Raquel might be coming down with it too. She looks shattered.

7.10 p.m. Commotion in kitchen. Uncle Albert's beard caught in food blender. Cut Albert free. Bin the blender.

8.00 p.m. Monkey Harris calls. Offers me first refusal on a shipment of Italian crocodile-effect loafers, made in Thailand. I tell him I'll be round first thing in the morning.

9.00 p.m. Rodney engrossed in a documentary about ozone layers and temperature changes. Raquel sparko.

10.00 p.m. Albert reminisces about the time a giant squid tried to nick his hat.

10.30 p.m. Nightcap. Cigar. Bog. Bed.

THE SECRET TO MY SUCCESS

And now for the bit you've all been waiting for ...

Ever since I hit the business seminar circuit, a lot of people have asked me what my secret is. '*How do you do it, Del?*' they say, their eyes filled with a mixture of awe and envy. '*Is there some sort of secret recipe to success?*' Usually I keep schtum. Not that I don't like to share, but come on, it would be like Paul Daniels telling you where he pulled the pigeon from. Plus you've always got to be careful not to give your competitors the edge.

Well, that was then, but *now*, exclusively for you, and by way of a simple diagram, I'm going to let you in on the secret.

I call it 'the Del Boy Paradigm'. What does paradigm mean? I dunno, but does it really matter? No. What matters is that it works. Allow me to explain how it all came about. Back in 2004 I decided to have one last crack at the motion-picture game. With my eye for a blockbuster and Rodney's natural flair for the written word (*The Indictment, There's a Rhino Loose in the City* and *The Island of Doom*, to name but a few of his works), it's an area TITCO has always been interested in.

Anyway, I managed to swing a meeting with a well-known movie producer. For legal reasons I can't give his name, but he was a member of Boycie's old Masonic lodge and I'd helped him out with an emergency Winnebago, so he owed me a favour. After a bit of a mare getting Boycie to arrange it – these Masons take their secrecy very seriously – this producer finally agreed to give me half an hour at his house (number 28 King's Avenue). Eager to exchange ideas, we settled down in his study to wax lyrical.

Before I knew it the half-hour had turned to an hour, and then to another, and he even brought out a carafe of port, it was going *that* well.

It was after the second carafe that we got into a heated debate about what was more important to a story, plot or character (the answer, by the way, is neither) and things took a sudden and ugly nosedive. I'm not proud of it so I won't go into detail, but during the course of the fight (it went on for just over twenty minutes) I took a smack in the eye from one of them ornamental paperweight things. To cut a short story even shorter, I ended up in A&E, and it was there, whilst sitting in the waiting room, that it came to me in a flash: the Del Boy Paradigm!

I quickly borrowed a notepad from the receptionist and with only one eye working and suffering what was later confirmed to be a mild percussion, I scribbled down my vision. What I ended up with was this:

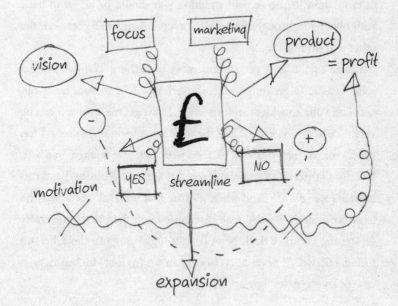

The Del Boy Business Paradigm™.

As you can see it's all very self-explanatory, so I won't waste my time or yours going into boring detail about what it all means; simply put, everything the modern-day businessman or woman needs to know is encapsulised in the paradigm. Don't believe me? Try it out for yourself. Just don't bother trying to pass it off as your own.*

I've already sorted the copyright.

BONJOUR

I'm afraid the time has come for me to tip my cap and bid you a fair ta-ta-for-now. If you've paid attention you should be all set to hack your own path through the jungle. I'm confident you'll come out the other end smiling.

Before I go, I want you to remember something: you don't ride a roller coaster to get somewhere, do yer? You do it so your heart can race and your knuckles can turn white. Don't get me wrong, it can be very nice to arrive, even if half the time it's not where you set off for, but it's the journey you look back on with a grin, or a laugh, or a tear. Usually all three. It's a game, you see, this life we call business and this business we call life. And while it's true that we've all gotta play the hand we're dealt, it's also true that more often than not some crafty git is using a marked deck. Now, I'm not suggesting you cheat, heaven forbid, but, well, it never hurts to keep an ace (or four) tucked away in case of emergencies. Just ask Boycie.

---

* People who lay claim to other people's ideas are really annoying.

I'll leave you now with a last-minute interview I managed to bribe out of Rodney ...

ME: *Right, you ready?*

RODNEY: *You know I don't like this, Del.*

ME: *It's all right, it won't take long. The book's almost finished, I just need a subtitle. It doesn't have to be fancy, just something that is unmistakably 'Del Boy'.*

RODNEY: *Short and simple.*

ME: *Exactly! I was thinking maybe something like* The Derek Trotter Guide to Market Penetration.

RODNEY: *Leave off, Del. You thought market penetration meant sex under a barrow.*

ME: *Rodney, you are sailing dangerously close to receiving a clump round the lughole. What's the matter with you? And why are you so reluctant to be involved in this book?*

RODNEY: *'Cos if it's anything like the last one I ain't gonna come out well in it.*

ME: *Don't worry, I won't embarrass you. I'll write nothing but nice things. I won't mention any of your ... little problems.*

RODNEY: *What little problems?*

ME: *I just said I won't mention 'em. Look, Rodders, I couldn't write* *a book like this and not include your voice, could I? You've been an integral part of the magic that is Trotters Independent Traders right from the off. You're the Boy Wonder to my Batman, the Tonto to my Lone Ranger, the Holly Wallaby to my Phillip Schofield!*

RODNEY: *Yeah, all right, I get the picture.*

ME: *I only want you to answer a few questions. The way you're talking it's like I'm asking you to pop over to India to climb Mount Everest!*

RODNEY: *Mount Everest is in China.*

ME: *This is no time for geography! I've got a book to write here.* Ménage a trois!

RODNEY: *Del, when are you gonna stop using these soppy French phrases? I've told you before, you can't speak French! You still ain't got the hang of English.*

ME: *The way things are going, Rodney, I'm going to have to terminate this interview.*

RODNEY: *Good!*

ME: *No, no, wait! Look, let's start with an easy one. What has been the highlight of your career?*

RODNEY: *When I was head of the computer section at Alan's printing firm.*

ME: *I meant your career with me.*

RODNEY: *Oh. Well ... I dunno, I'll have to get back to you on that one.*

ME: *Fair enough. On the flip side, do you have any regrets?*

RODNEY: *Bloody hell, loads!*

ME: *OK, let's move on ...*

RODNEY: *I had high hopes for myself when I was a kid.*

ME: *Yeah, well, we all did.*

RODNEY: *I could've been someone and made something of my life. I could've had my own business and been my own boss; I could've been a successful novelist or travelled the world making my name as an artist ... I could've been on* Top of the Pops!

ME: *Blimey, you make it sound as though you wish you'd never joined the firm.*

RODNEY: *Well ...*

ME: *Well?*

RODNEY: *Of course I don't mean that ... I just mean ... you know.*

[Pause.]

ME: *We did have some laughs though, didn't we?*

RODNEY: *Yeah, there were a good few along the way.*

ME: *'Ere, d'you remember that time on the beach in Benidorm when I put that crab in Grandad's hat?*

RODNEY: *Yeah, he didn't have a clue, did he?*

ME: *Not a scooby. All day long he had it on.*

RODNEY: *His face when he took it off to go to bed. He was so shocked his teeth fell out.*

ME: *I just wish I'd had my Polaroid ready.*

[Pause.]

ME: *I did my best, Rodney.*

RODNEY: *I know you did, bruv.*

ME: *And look on the bright side, you might not have done or been any of those things you mentioned, but at the very least you've always had your big brother at your side to help guide you.*

RODNEY: *I can't argue with that.*

ME: *Good boy. You know it makes sense.*

Lovely Jubbly!

LINGO GUIDE

★★★★★★★★★★★★★★★★★★★★★★

For those of you unfamiliar with the cockney vernacular, in this case, Peckhamese, here're a few translations you might find useful:

Adam and Eve
Meaning: believe
Usage: 'Would you Adam and Eve it?'

April
Meaning: arse
Usage: 'My old April was going like the clappers!'

bandy (knocked)
Meaning: impressing someone, particularly a woman
Usage: 'A bit of French always knocks 'em bandy.'

barney
Meaning: a heated argument
Usage: 'I had a right barney with Raquel last night.'

bird
Meaning: woman
Usage: 'I'm a geezer, I'm not a bird.'

blinding
Meaning: great, smashing, top-notch
Usage: 'Say what you like about the French but they make a blinding bottle of plonk!'

blower
Meaning: phone
Usage: ''Ere, have a butchers at my new mobile blower.'
Also: dog and bone

brown bread
Meaning: dead
Usage: 'That canary is well
and truly brown bread!'

bunse
Meaning: money/
a nice little earner
Usage: 'There's nothing I like
more than making a lovely bit
of bunse!'

butchers
Meaning: look
Usage: *See* blower

cobblers
Meaning: rubbish
Usage: 'Don't give me all that
old cobblers!'
Also: pony

cop/copping
Meaning: getting/taking
Usage: 'Keep on like this,
Rodney, and you'll cop an
unfortunate one!'

cream-crackered
Meaning: knackered/tired
Usage: 'After a long hard day
in the city I feel absolutely
cream-crackered.'

cushty
Meaning: good/nice/easy
Usage: 'This ain't bad.
This is cushty.'
Also: lovely jubbly

dipstick
Meaning: a foolish person
Usage: 'Don't be a dipstick all
your life, Rodney.'
Also: dippy

doddle
Meaning: easy/a piece of cake
Usage: 'It's not difficult, it's an
absolute doddle!'

dozy
Meaning: slow
Usage: 'You dozy twonk!'

face-ache

Meaning: a very bad mood

Usage: 'I'd steer clear of Raquel if I were you, she's got the right face-ache!'

Also: hump, needle

filbert

Meaning: head

Usage: 'Use your filbert.'

Also: noddle, bonce

flog/flogged

Meaning: to sell something

Usage: 'Leave it out, Rodders, you couldn't flog lettuce to a rabbit.'

Also: outed, knocked out

geezer

Meaning: man

Usage: 'I'm a bird, I'm not a geezer.'

Also: bloke, mush

Gok Wong

Meaning: wrong

Usage: 'Bloody hell, it's all gone Gok Wong!'

Also: belly-up, tits-up, gone for a burton

gubbins

Meaning: miscellaneous stuff/info

Usage: 'We don't need to muck about with warranties and guarantees and all that old gubbins.'

Also: gumf

half-inched

Meaning: stolen

Usage: 'He half-inched it down the market.'

Also: hooky, knocked off

Hobson's

Meaning: voice

Usage: 'After a particularly loud day in the market, nothing rejuvenates the old Hobson's like an ice-cold pina colada.'

hooter

Meaning: nose

Usage: 'Stop picking your hooter!'

Humpty-Dumpty

Meaning: sexual intracourse

Usage: 'Fancy a bit of Humpty-Dumpty?'

Also: doink

Jacobs

Meaning: male generatalia

Usage: 'To succeed in business, there are times when you've gotta lay your Jacobs on the line.'

Also: balls, knackers, goolies, plums, nuts, family jewels, doo-dahs, giblets, two-veg, domesticles, rungles, right-said-Freds, spud-bunkers, testinads, dim-sum sacks, steam pouch, scrotch eggs, Mitchell brothers*

khazi

Meaning: toilet

Usage: 'I'll call you back in five minutes. I've just this second sat down on the khazi.'

Also: bog, Kermit

kibosh

Meaning: to end something

Usage: 'The advent of email stuck the kibosh on the fax machine.'

kip

Meaning: to sleep

Usage: 'I don't know about you but I'm cream-crackered. I'm going for a kip.'

knackered

See cream-crackered

lugholes

Meaning: ears

Usage: 'Gordon Bennett! Cop a load of the lugholes on that mush!'

---

* I ain't heard of half of these, but Damien assures me they're pukka.

lumber/lumbered
Meaning: a predicament
Usage: 'I'm in dead lumber!'
Also: schtook

mince pies
Meaning: eyes
Usage: 'At these prices you
won't believe your mince pies.'

moby
See dipstick

monkey
Meaning: five hundred quid
Usage: 'This'll cost you a
monkey up west. I'm letting it
go for a pony.'

mooey
Meaning: face
Usage: 'That bloke is sailing
dangerously close to copping
a smack in the mooey!'
Also: boat race

mutton
Meaning: deaf
Usage: 'You should clean
your lugholes out, mate.
You've gone mutton!'

nause
Meaning: to ruin
something/something ruined
Usage: 'You've naused that right
up, you plonker!'
Also: cock-up, balls-up, belly-
up, tits-up, gone for a burton

Nelson Riddle
Meaning: urinate (piddle)
Usage: 'Hold that thought,
I'm just going for
a Nelson Riddle.'
Also: Jimmy Riddle, spend
a penny, slash

nicker
Meaning: one pound
Usage: 'It retails at £5.99
but you can have it for a nicker!'
Also: a note, sov, quid

nipper
Meaning: child
Usage: 'Boycie was one weird-looking nipper.'
Also: sprog

paddy (throw a)
Meaning: have a minor breakdown
Usage: 'All right, calm down, Denzil, don't throw a paddy!'
Also: doing his/her pieces

pear-shaped
Meaning: wonky/ruined
Usage: 'Blimey, it's all gone pear-shaped.'
Also: naused, cock-up, balls-up, belly-up, tits-up, gone for a burton

pen and ink
Meaning: stink
Usage: 'Stone me, it don't 'alf pen and ink in here. Have you dropped one, Grandad?'

plonker
See moby

pony
Meaning: crap
Usage: 'Don't give me all that old pony!'
Also: twenty-five nicker
Usage: 'I'm down to my last pony.'

porky pies
Meaning: lies
Usage: 'As important as it is to be honest and upfront with people, the occasional little porky pie never hurt anyone.'

pukka
Meaning: good/genuine
Usage: 'This ain't pony. This is pukka.'
Also: kosher

readies
Meaning: money
Usage: 'Sorry, Rodney, I'm temporarily out of readies.'
Also: bunse, dosh, dough, spondulicks, wad

Ruby Murray
Meaning: curry
Usage: 'I say, this Ruby Murray is rather spicy.'

schtum
Meaning: to keep quiet
Usage: 'Keep schtum and nobody will be any the wiser.'

scooby
Meaning: clue
Usage: 'Honestly, I didn't have a scooby!'

skint
Meaning: out of money
Usage: 'I'm so skint, the ducks are throwing bread at me.'
Also: potless, brassic

sort
Meaning: an attractive woman
Usage: 'Look at that bird. What a sort!'
Also: brahma

stone me
Meaning: exclamation
Usage: 'Stone me, what a cushty book this is.'
Also: Gordon Bennett, blimey

syrup
Meaning: a wig
Usage: 'Look at the state of that bloke's syrup. Who does he think he is, Davy Crockett?'

tart
Meaning: someone who moans/a whiner
Usage: 'What are you going on about, you tart?!'

Toby (taking a)
Meaning: a leisurely stroll
Usage: 'I think I'll leave the
van and take a nice Toby.'
Also: mosey

tom-dick
Meaning: sick
Usage: 'Witnessing childbirth
can make a lot of blokes feel
a bit tom-dick. I was all right
'cos I used to run a jellied
eel stall.'

tom-tit
Meaning: what results
from a bowel movement
Usage: 'Thanks to Rodney, we
are now knee-deep in tom-tit!'
Also: Eartha Kitt, two-bob-bit,
Richard the Third

twonk
See plonker

wally
See twonk

INDEX

★★★★★★★★★★★

Page references in *italics* indicate images.